Working With the Merlin

Geoff Hughes

Working With the Merlin

ISBN 1 86163 001 8

ALL RIGHTS RESERVED

Cover design by Paul Mason

Published by:

Capall Bann Publishing
Freshfields
Chieveley
Berks
RG20 8TF

Contents

Chapter 1

Our Heritage - The Merlin of the Past

Many people ask who, or what, is The Merlin? There are many ideas as to the answers to these simple questions. Each is equally valid and all I can do is offer the information that I have been given. To set the scene for today we need first of all to look back into the past to find the foundation from which we are Working. No one is in any real position to offer any scientific concrete evidence to prove or disprove what follows. It is based on personal 'input' received from those Unseen Guardians and Teachers in the rarefied strata's of the multi-dimensions and inner planes of our physical world.

Firstly, back through the Mists of Time, to the Island of Rhuta, the Capital and central pivot of the Island Lands of Atlantis. The Kingdom of Atlantis derived its power from the transmutation of Off-World Energies with those of the Earth through a mighty Crystal, which was housed in the major 'Sun Temple', on a plateau atop the mountain in the centre of Rhuta. The men and women of the Priesthood tended the Temple and its Crystal with the utmost devotion and reverence. There were no human sacrifices to Sun Gods, etc.; just an all pervading joy in service to the One God, Who is All Gods. Depending on the aptitude of the Priests and Priestesses, each mediated a particular 'vibration' on behalf of the Land and its People. Some were, therefore, Mediators to the Moon, the Sun, the Sea, the Earth, etc.. They wore simple robes, mainly of white with a simple tie about forehead and waist which was colour coded to the Energy that they Worked with.

1

Utilising their knowledge of Crystal and its properties they directed the Crystal Energy into the many homes and offices throughout the Empire to fuel their communications, household and every day needs.

Once Atlantis reached the height of its power and influence, it could evolve no further. The then High Priestess, Meera, and the High Priest, Menya, knew that it was the beginning of the end. They knew that they were the last of the 'true' Priesthood and in the time yet to follow, their successors would develop the downfall and destruction of the Atlantean culture. But it wasn't all doom and gloom. They knew that far, far into their future new Priests and Priestesses would rise to rekindle the basis of the Atlantean culture and to bring a new, evolved system to the planet. The future problem would be that the then men and women of the Priesthood would only have a vague, dim, distant, spiritual memory of the Atlantean process of balancing Energies to create harmony within the Planet. Menya and Meera knew that there would be no way that they could leave a physical guidance system that would survive the destruction and still be in a readily accessible and comprehensible form so far in their future. The two of them quietly set themselves to finding a way to link with the future. Sometimes alone, sometimes together, sometimes utilising the entire Priesthood, they found a way.

Spiralling the multi-dimensions they set up 'milestones', 'marker-posts' along the many Time Lines of the Future. Messages imprinted in Time and Space for those who would follow. They knew that this was 'safe' because only those with the innate abilities would be able to find, read and understand these imprints sufficiently to carry the Work further along its evolution. The future would be founded solely on the personal abilities of the individual and not on academia nor politics. It wouldn't matter if a person could read or write, was athletic, a couch potato, or physically disabled, clever or simple. If they had the ability they would find the 'message' and they would know and understand what was required of them.

All through this endeavour Menya and Meera maintained a close liaison with the Inner Planes and Worked with them in setting

2

things up for the long term future of the Earth. In due course, when all was ready, Menya and Meera died. The memory of their efforts passed and was forgotten. The end grew nearer until one day the then Priesthood realised that they could alter the way of Working within the Sun Temple and, they thought, stave off the day of destruction. They endeavoured to reorientate the Crystal Power to other means. It is unclear, and unnecessary to know, what this aim was. Suffice it to say that they attempted it.

Some however were fully aware that the end of Atlantis could not be halted. In an attempt to retain the essential elements of their Way of Life these priests and priestesses arranged a Colonisation Programme for Expansion. Volunteers were called for an expedition to settle the Western Lands and they set forth, taking with them, naturally, representatives of the Priesthood to care for the explorers, to be their High Priestess and High Priest, and to carry the knowledge with them in order for it to survive. Time passed and the Atlanteans lost interest and contact was broken with the migrants. A further expedition was then mounted, but this time to head towards the East, the West having been considered a failure. The migration repeated itself inasmuch as the Priesthood travelled again for the same reasons. This journey was even longer than the previous one and contact was lost almost immediately. Time was running out.

A third and final migration was hurriedly gathered together and they were bundled aboard a single ship. On board were a Priest of the Moon and a Sea Priestess, chosen to be the colony's High Priest and Priestess. There was no decision made as to where they were to go; there just wasn't time. Three days out, looking astern, the migrants saw a cloud of darkness on the far horizon. There was no time to grieve. Crew and passengers leapt to their feet and frantically prepared the ship to ride out the coming tidal-wave. And come it did, with a vengeance. For days the ship was flung from billow to billow, often in dire straits, never far from totally floundering. Any pretence at following a specified course had been blown to the winds.

As with all things, it eventually came to an end and the seas calmed. Battered, bruised and sickened the migrants began to take stock of their surroundings. To starboard there were inhospitable cliffs, pounded by the ocean rollers, without, it appeared, any suitable landing area. It was decided to keep heading generally towards the North, following the coastline until they should chance upon a suitable landing site. Two days later, in deep water off the coastline, they became aware of the fact that they were in real trouble with a lack of drinking water and cliffs or not they would have to make a landing.

Fortune smiled upon them and a small beach with scaleable cliffs hove into view. Thankfully they landed in what was to be their new home-land. After many attempts they finally managed to get everyone up onto the cliff tops, where they discovered that there was an indigenous population of semi-nomadic people. They were received courteously and before long were accepted into the Tribe. A relationship soon developed, as each learnt from the other, as their tenets were found to be compatible. The Atlanteans learnt that there were many of these tribes scattered throughout the land, but each tribe was bound by treaty to a specified area of the country and they remained in their own areas. After a few weeks of travelling and resting, the tribe came to a region of small islands in a vast lakeland area. The homesick Atlantean contingent asked if they could be granted permission to settle and colonise these islands. Discussion with the tribal elders ensued and the plan was accepted. The tribe moved on, leaving the Atlanteans to sort themselves out.

They settled quickly and soon became a sizeable community. Word of their settlement gradually spread throughout the land. Tribal elders from the other semi-nomadic people expressed the desire to meet and talk with the newcomers and the word was passed back to the community. Here was a new concept for the Atlantean Priest and Priestess. Heretofore they had always remained in their temple and those who sought them knew where to find them. But these were new conditions in a new environment and required adaptations to be made. After lengthy considerations it was decided that the High Priestess would remain in the community, whilst the High Priest was given a roving commission to travel the land, meeting the tribal elders, teaching and learning, but with the injunction to return to the community for each Winter period. He was also encouraged to seek out prospective candidates for the future Priests and Priestesses, and to send them back to the islands for training.

The system worked well for a number of years, the community settled into a routine and the knowledge spread throughout the land. Candidates duly arrived for training and ordination. In the fullness of time the original High Priest and High Priestess died and were replaced by suitable successors, and the wheel continued to turn with the passing of time, and new High Priests and Priestesses were selected as required.

Early one Spring, word was received in the community of the arrival of a new group of people on the land's shores. The High Priest was despatched forthwith to meet and greet these newcomers and to invite them back to the community if they so wished to come, and come they did, were made welcome and were soon accepted into the priesthood. The tenets were, once again, found to be very compatible and blended well. Over the next couple of hundred years things continued pleasantly, but evolution required movement. Schism erupted, basic tenets were 'adjusted' to meet the changing face of Life and the Ways of Men; they lost the original theme. One broke away from the other, setting up a separate establishment in close proximity to the first. The First Battle for the Hearts and Minds of the Populace was launched. It was a long and sorry to say bloody exchange, which produced nothing. A halt was called, finally, because a war-like invader was crossing the Eastern Sea, bent on raping, pillaging and looting. Previously invaders had landed and, after a little adjustment, had settled without any undue problems; allowing the religions to flourish as they would. A truce was called between the two factions in order to meet this foe with a common front and a search was instigated throughout the land for a common war leader to lead the armies against the invader; thereby dissolving the centuries old treaties of each to their own part of the land.

One was eventually found in the person of a tribal chieftain, Uther. The High Priesthood of both the major factions joined his War Cabinet to give their aid to the war effort. In order to differentiate between them the two sects chose names to identify their Leaders. One was called the equivalent of today's 'Archbishop', whilst the other was known as 'The Merlin'. A Priestess was quickly trained to undertake the roving commission of the Merlin, since he now had other duties to occupy his time, and she was despatched into the land. She chose to call herself Morgana, meaning 'from the Sea'. The High Priestess became known as The Lady of the Lake. The Merlin and The Lady of the Lake together produced the magical battle sword Excalibur for King Arthur; the aim of the sword was to fight and weld the diverse, petty kingdoms into a single unity.

The rest of that story lies hidden in the Legends of the Arthuriad. But, even more hidden was the fact that The Merlin, The Lady and the King used the magic of Excalibur to turn OFF certain Earth energies throughout the land of Albion. Across the World other Magicians and Shamen did exactly the same thing, in their own ways, for their own Lands. Evolution demanded that mankind needed to undergo a period of gross materialism.

(So far, no-one has given me what I would really call an adequate answer as to why mankind needed this particular situation in order for the continuance of the march of evolution. Perhaps, one day, someone will tell me?)

With the ending of hostilities in Britain, peace began to settle on the land. The two factions prepared to return to the battle for their individual existence's, and supremacy over the peoples, but The Merlin refused to allow any further hostilities and disbanded his Priesthood; offering them the opportunity to join the other faction or to return to their homes. It is unclear how the Lady of the Lake and Morgana took this, but legend has it that they wove a mist to conceal their island home in Avallon, down in the Summer County, and those still drawn to the 'old ways', will find them there. Legend tells us that there was a Final Battle and that King Arthur was mortally wounded. He despatched one of his surviving Knights of the Round Table to return Excalibur to The Lady of the Lake, whereupon King Arthur was taken by three unidentified ladies on a royal barge across the sea to Ynys Writtin (The Isle of Glass) to be healed of his wounds and to, supposedly, await his Country's Call. The Merlin, himself, disappeared into obscurity once his task was done, and, the legend tells us, took himself off to a cave where he sealed himself away and slept until the day he was needed again - when Britain stood in peril. Whilst The Merlin kept his watchful sleep the Inquisition and the Witch-hunts came to hold the course of Evolution steady; to bury mankind in the physical, material world as required in the longer term.

Across the Atlantic in Hydesville, New York State, on March 31st, 1848, two sisters, Margaretta and Catherine Fox, dared to communicate with a Charles B. Rosna, a deceased peddler, who had been murdered and buried in the cellar of their home in 1843. The way of Spiritual Contact (channelling) was 'rediscovered' and so what is now known as Modern Spiritualism was born, crossing the ocean to Britain in 1850, to be met with prejudice, bigotry and intolerance at all levels.

Towards the end of the 19th Century the public imagination became fired by the excavations of the Tombs of the Pharaohs in Egypt. Archaeologists and philosophers bent their minds and talents to the mighty task of understanding the early Egyptians, with varying degrees of success. Some people, unable to accept the pundit's view, began their own researches; but turned from the physical to the metaphysical world for their answers. Temples and Fraternities sprang up all over Great Britain as men and women strove to re-establish contact with the Inner Planes and those who, it was hoped, could give answers to the many imponderable questions which were constantly arising.

Most notable amongst these was the Order of the Golden Dawn which brought together many of the great names in the Esoteric World, even though they were never all members, necessarily, at the same time. Aliester Crowley, MacGregor Mathers, and Violet Mary Firth. Violet who? Within the Lodge people shrugged off their physical persona and became known by their spiritual aspiration. Violet chose to be known as DNF, which was a shortened way of aspiring towards 'Deo Non Fortuna' - 'God, not Fate'. As her writings took hold so the name became Dion Fortune. At the appropriate time in her life she came away from the Golden Dawn and set up her own Teaching School, the Society of the Inner Light, which taught the basics of the Hebraic Qabalah and how to make contact with the Inner Planes. The Course of Instruction completed successful applicants were often invited to join the inner Lodge; the Fraternity of the Inner Light. There they wove their magic towards the Regeneration of Mankind.

A few years before the Second World War two of the members, Colonel Kim Seymour and Christine Hartley, left the Fraternity and began to Work on their own together. They made contact with an Inner Plane Teacher that they came to know as Cheiron, who then passed them on to the stirring Merlin Energy of Britain.

In 1936 an aircraft designer by the name of Mitchell was commissioned by the then Ministry of Aviation to design an aircraft around a prototype engine that had been designed by Messrs Rolls and Royce. Suffice it to say he did so and produced the Spitfire and Hurricane fighter planes. In September 1939 came the Battle for Britain. These little aircraft and their pilots, battled their way to supremacy of the skies over England; averting the threatened invasion by the Third Reich. The name given to the engine right from inception? Merlin. As well as being used in these fighters, the engines were also used in Lancaster's, Mosquitoes and Halifax's. Additionally, Britain negotiated with the United States of America for Mustangs under Lease/Lend. On arrival the aircraft's Packard engines were inspected and modified by the Merlin engineers. It could be argued philosophically therefore, that The Merlin awoke and came to Britain's aid in Her Darkest Hour; in fulfilment of the Legend/Prophecy.

Esoterically, the whole of 'Magical Britain' individually, but physically unconnected, wove a Psychic Shield across the English Channel against the very real threat of an invasion.

The various aircraft propelled by the Merlin engines became the modern Swords wielded by the few modern Knights. The Spirit of Excalibur, driven by The Merlin Energy, carried the Pilot/Knights, with the Spirit of King Arthur and the Knights of the Round Table in their blood, in the Final Defence of the Land.

Dion passed from earthly toil in 1946 and, some little while after her passing, the Fraternity of the Inner Light found it necessary to perform a cleansing ritual within the Lodge to remove her influence in order that it too should continue to evolve.

After heavy persecution the British Spiritualist's spearheaded the Repeal of the Witchcraft Act in the early 1950s. For years their Mediums had been arraigned before the Justices with prostitutes and murderers simply for practising their religion. With that repeal such things as Wicca were once again allowed to flourish. Britain was beginning to get back into the metaphysical World.

Chapter Two

My Merlin Contact

Having encompassed a millennia or two in a page or so it is necessary to ease up and introduce myself. I was born Geoffrey Howard Hughes on January 14, 1943, in Lewisham, Southeast London. In the 1950s my parents divorced; a rarity in those days and not socially acceptable. Turbulent schooling followed, resulting in my finishing my education without any qualifications; due probably to my own inability to accept the family situation. Two years after leaving school I enlisted in the British Army, joining the Royal Corps of Signals. This was possibly an omen of things to come. The cap badge and symbol of the Corps is the wing footed figure of Hermes, Messenger of the Gods. There was a lot of service in Germany, plus time in Borneo, Singapore and Ulster. I achieved the rank of Sergeant and finished my twenty two years service as an Army Careers Information Officer (Recruiter) in Southend on Sea in 1983.

In 1964 I had married and we had raised three children. An ordinary, unremarkable guy.

I am none too sure as to when my actual metaphysical life started. I have a distant, yet persistent, memory of being about eight or nine in the early 50s. My 'craze' was to take a dried milk tin, punch a hole in the bottom, insert a light fitting, wire up a long length of twin flex plugged into the mains and stand in my grand-mother's garden at night sweeping the beam across the night sky. I'm here, where are you?

It really took hold of me in September 1968 when I returned to England from the Far East with a large amount of leave accrued. I found a small Spiritualist's Church in Katherine Street,

Doncaster, Yorkshire, and began to attend Services and Open Development Circles. The latter are open to anyone to sit, under the guidance of a Medium, to develop whatever psychic/spiritual ability is latent in them. I had become intrigued at the concept of being able to communicate with those who were deemed to have died. I could do that! I set out to prove it. I discovered the rudimentary ability to 'see' the unseen worlds about me; clairvoyance. 'The Dream' for me was to become a Medium; to participate in the mandate of Spiritualism. Prove the Survival of the Individuality beyond the state known as Death. I could not think of anything else, at that time, that could be more important than the removal of the fear of death carried by us all.

Whenever I got back to England on leave or courses I haunted the nearest Spiritualist's church. Meeting myriad people of varying degrees of sensitivity. They came and went, always leaving their mark on my questing mind. Abroad and out of contact with mediums and such like I came across a number of Esoteric Schools that ran correspondence courses. In turn I joined a number of them in the Quest for Knowledge and Experience. Some of the courses I completed, but soon found that that particular school had nothing further to offer. Some I left because it didn't take long to realise that they only worshipped Mammon; the great silver dollar. Others were left because it became obvious that they were not a part of my 'Path'; I didn't fit in. But I was always learning; sometimes finding out what not to do, which is equally important.

In 1976 I threw it all up and turned to fencing and archery. I had become disillusioned with the pettiness of 'Great Aunt Freda brings you a lovely bunch of flowers'; 'they tell me that you're under a dark cloud at the moment but this will pass and Spirit are doing all they can to help you at this time'. I found that I was saying the same thing time after time after time. I had lost the 'buzz'. I had received my 'proof' over the years as those deceased that I knew of came back to advise me of their continuance beyond the veil.

Two years later I found the book *The Mystical Qabalah* by Dion Fortune, which led me into the course and on into the Fraternity of the Inner Light to become an Initiate of the Western Mystery Tradition. A few years later the Inner Planes Grand Master of the Lodge instructed me to leave the Lodge; fly solo and Work with The Merlin Energy of Britain. Petulantly I had finally given in and had settled under his tutorship and was moved into the Worlds of the Tarot, Spiritual Healing, the Native American Medicine Wheel, Wicca, and Working with National and Planetary Energies. Under the guidance of The Merlin and his feminine counterpart, the Lady of the Lake, I revitalised the National Energy, known to me as the Pendragon. I told how this Working was achieved when I co-authored the book, *Ancient Magicks for a New Age*, with Alan Richardson, published in 1989 by Llewellyn Publications of St Paul, Minnesota.

Whilst I was involved in the Pendragon Work, The Merlin showed me a vision, instructing me to bring it into physical manifestation. This is only notable inasmuch as in the general scheme of magical things a magician has an object and then creates an energy field about it. Here I was presented with an energy and told to find a suitable receptacle for it. Over many years, and with the help of many people who came and went in my life, it was finally accomplished and manifested as the Masculine Dragon Sword which has been used on a variety of occasions to the benefit of the Lands and the Planet. No-one owns the Dragon Sword, I am simply its Custodian.

The Merlin Energy advised me that the time had come for the revitalisation of those long closed Earth Energies; to turn them ON again. Under Inner Plane guidance I, with others, began the process of doing so in England, and this was finally accomplished on June 21, 1991 at approximately 4.45 in the morning at the hidden sacred henge of Arbor Low in Derbyshire, using the Dragon Sword and it's energies.

Divorced, I met and eventually married my wife June, a Certificated Speaker and Demonstrator of the Spiritualist's National Union of Great Britain and is, currently, the Regional Training Officer for the Union for the East and Southeast of England.

In February, 1993, we received an invitation from the Spiritual Research Association of Iceland in Reykjavik to spend some time with them. Our reputation as Readers and Healers quickly spread and we started Teaching Workshops on a variety of subjects. With the permission of the Icelandic Inner Planes Guardians, we also moved around the icy wastes, stimulating Earth Energies through the Dragon Sword, which accompanies us everywhere we go, in accordance with the original mandate set by the Merlin.

Back in England, the Feminine Moon Sword came into our possession. Forged by an unknown Lady who was knowledgeable in the Sacred Ways more than a century ago. The Two Swords became aligned and now Work together.

Our horizons widened and we, with the Two Swords, found ourselves in the United States of America, Working and assisting people in the re-activation of the Earth Energies of that Land, even spending a little time with the Native Americans on a Reservation. We returned to the United Kingdom having been adopted as Grandparent Teachers of the Wolf Clan of the Rainbow Tribe of the Lakota Sioux.

So much for me; what about The Merlin?

He is not a man. The name is derived from the appointment, much as some countries have a President, or Monarch. In this case it is a Masculine Energy. An energy for Britain. To a limited degree the Energy can be contacted in other countries, but with nothing like the force and power that he radiates in his homeland; but that will be discussed in greater detail in later pages. The Merlin appears to a large number of people in different guises. I wish it to be strictly understood that I lay no claims to being the only one to have such a contact; I know of many others who have made a similar contact.

As far as I am aware, and he has never given any indication to the contrary, he very, very rarely appears in the Spiritualist environment. He once muttered something about not being dead.

There is a particular, symbolic picture that he presents to me clairvoyantly. There is the 'feeling' that accompanies this vision that 'tells' me it is not my mind playing tricks on me. It is very difficult to explain; it is a 'knowing'. There can be, under these circumstance, absolutely no question that it is him. I admit that on many occasions when I have requested to speak to him I have only been aware of my own impression of his presence, but, when he considers it is sufficiently important he makes darn sure that I will not be in any doubt that he is there.

He has appeared as the Disney version (see *The Sword in the Stone)*, as the Boorman portrayal (see *Excalibur*) and often as either a patch of amethyst colour or a similarly coloured vortex of force. The 'uncertainty' of how he will appear can add a little zest to the contact. You expect one thing and something the opposite turns up.

His self portrayal in human form can be much like the Rider-Waite Tarot Card, The Hermit. It is in the guise of a monkish style habit, with hood, drawstring at the waist, but with long flowing 'wings' from ankles to wrists, so that when he raises his 'arms' the movement is emphasised by the sweep of the cloth. Naturally, he is bearded, but the eyes defy description. He quite often, but not always, carries a staff, almost as tall as himself, totally plain without embellishment.

In essence The Merlin is the wisdom of all the time and energy that is Great Britain.

There is a distinct and very severe streak of sternness. He can be extremely caustic, refuses to suffer fools gladly and can be extremely rude, even though on rare occasions, he can and does laugh with a bright, merry sense of humour. Unfortunately, this does not happen very often.

He is a stern taskmaster, who drives hard, not because he wants to but because he has to. He is infinitely patient when he appreciates that I am doing my limited best on his behalf. He is constantly impressing on me that time is short (for what I am not sure) and that we must buckle down to the job in hand.

14

At this point I was going to spend some time endeavouring to set out some of the many philosophical points that he has taught me, but no matter how I wrote it, it still kept looking as if I was saying what a jolly clever chap I am. That is not what this is about.

The Merlin's method of teaching is to plant a seed thought in the conscious mind, disappear and leave you to sort it out. Some while later he will check in with you to see how you have got on with the idea. If it is not quite right he will mutter something encouraging like a gruff 'do it again' and disappear. When he is satisfied there'll be a terse 'okay', and that is it until the next time.

He maintains that we need all the people we can muster, but, above all, they must be willing volunteers, without coercion, who are willing to serve their lands. It is the world-wide situation that needs rectification and restoring which can only be resolved through people, ordinary people, being prepared to act as catalysts.

Chapter 3

Answers

Before we become involved in the technicalities of the Work that we shall be undertaking, let us just sit awhile and chew things over and take a look at some of the questions that are often asked about Esoteric Work. Just because I am writing these pages, hopefully, under the guidance of my mentor does not make them inviolate and devoid of error; nor are they written in letters of fire on tablets of stone. No way! I am a human being on my particular path and am just as prone to fall flat on my face as anybody else. I speak from experience. My nose has been flattened on many occasions as it has made contact with dust or concrete. Not so much now, of course. The middle age spread has spread a little further and I only rock on it with a faint chance of the nose coming into contact.

All that follows arises from contact with those on the Inner Planes (irreverently known to us as 'input' from 'The Management') and my own experiences in either thinking through the idea given or carrying out any tasks that have been assigned, and mixing in, I hope, a little common sense.

On a number of occasions the question was asked as to why they just couldn't give out the answer. The response was always the same. Learning by Discovery. The answer is always accepted more readily if we have had to work it out for ourselves.

One of the early concepts bounced off of me produced the following realisation. Each one of us is an incarnate Spirit, which has chosen to descend into the Physical Realm in order to undergo Physical Experiences, therefore we should look to the Physical Realm of our choice. The argument is that, having elected to come here, we should concentrate on here. Learn from all the lessons and experiences that come our way. We should fully acknowledge this World and live in it. Many people seem to be under the assumption that we should live 'Spiritual' lives. Based on the ideas received so far, that is far from being the true case. We have selected a physical life therefore live physically; by all means, however, have an understanding of the ways of the Other Worlds and Planes. None of us are here to be Spiritual. We are here to be Physical. If we were supposed to be Spiritual it could be argued that we would still be in the, so called, Spiritual Worlds.

We are always being asked for an explanation of what exactly 'Magic' is and of what use it is?. Whilst it may seem very straight forward to anyone who has dealings with such, when we try to get it over to others we get stuck. I, no less than any other. I believe that it can best be defined by the idea of Cause and Effect. We constantly see this in the normal everyday life. You put the crockery in the sink, add water and soap, mix, and you end up with clean plates. Cause and Effect.

In the same way, an idea is sent onto the other levels in the knowledge that a desired outcome will result. Only it tends to be much more subtle in the way of working. A Magician sends the required concept 'upstairs' to the other planes, then walks away and forgets that they ever did it. Secure in the knowledge that the required result will manifest itself in the fullness of time. You start at point A, looking to arrive, eventually, at point Z. How the thing gets between the two points is of no consequence. To my cost I have found that it is pointless to try and follow it through; to see how it is going. Invariably the route is totally alien to any ideas of how we thought it would go. Point Z does arrive; eventually!

A thought that needs to be born in mind is that anything that is created by magic must be sustained by magic. In other words, the old Witches' Love Potion, Charm or Spell will only Work for so long; invariably a complete Moon Phase. Thereafter it will disappear and its effects will wear off, unless the whole thing is repeated, and repeated, and repeated. If you've nothing else to do with your life, fine. If you do have something else to do, it soon gets neglected under the press of other matters. So, what's the point? In the Cosmic Scheme of Things, so to speak, things are a touch different. The Magician is coming from a different point of perspective. How Billy and Jenny get on together is not, really, going to have too much effect on the Evolution of Planet Earth and its role within the Solar System and the Cosmos. For a start, the 'eye of newt', 'dragon's blood' and such don't figure.

Its all about the use of the mind of the Magician. They use their mind to move into an altered state of consciousness and, through this, contact another octave of vibration, which is probably best explained by considering Water. At extremely low temperature we have solid ice. Raise the temperature and we have liquid water. Raise it more and we have gaseous steam, and then up further to 'super' steam. All these have the same molecular structure, but each are operating on a different 'frequency'.

Having achieved this other vibrational contact within the mind, what are we actually going to do? There are no hard and fast rules. What is required lies totally in the hands, or mind, of the Magician and those with whom they are in contact. Which brings us to the ideas of Black Magic and White Magic. What's the difference? Everybody knows that! Black is evil and white is good. Is this really so? From who's point of view? I might see somebody doing something that is, to my mind, evil, but to them it is the exact opposite. Okay, I don't mean beating up old ladies and such, but things on a more personal level, such as paddling the seat of an errant youngster. Who can be the judge? Quite often we only see a snapshot of any given situation. We have not seen the events that led up to the paddling, nor may we see the outcome. We have no knowledge of the Cause which created the paddling Effect. How can we condemn? Except by jumping to conclusions based on uncertain facts and our own philosophy.

Once again, experience talking. I spent some years physically working with two police forces; both on the Reception Desk and as a Controller (Despatcher). My job included taking the first call for assistance and sending a unit, or units, to the scene. Invariably the actual incident had little or no relation to the actuality reported. Up to twenty people may have seen the incident, but no two of them will agree over what is, or was, going on. Who said what to whom or in who did what to whom in the first place. Many simply saw an out of focus snapshot and leapt. To quote from *The Pirates of Penzance* by Gilbert and Sullivan; 'a policeman's lot is not a happy one'.

Originally I was, like many, under the impression that Black Magic was about Working magic for ourselves, whilst White was for the benefit of others. Let me tell you, there are very, very few saints around these days. A certain well known philanthropist who works very hard for the benefit of the poor refuses to go anywhere unless they fly First Class. Any magical action can be justified in the longer term; depending on the point of view held.

In the movie, *The King and I*, the King of Siam speaks of understanding things as right and things as not, but, as he matured he found that things were often nearly so, nearly not. 'Tis a puzzlement!

In my own mind I have come to accept that, perhaps, I am a Grey Magician. I make errors of judgement the same as everyone else. I let my emotions, sometimes, get in the way and cloud my reasoning. I'm learning though! Emotions have a very strong tendency to interfere with the contact with the Mentor; whoever it may be.

A Magician may have an idea, but, if they are worth anything, the Magician will do absolutely nothing until they have been to check it; entered an altered state of consciousness; made contact with their mentor; discussed it; come back and thought it over some more; taken it back to their mentor, and so on, until there is complete agreement on the actions, if any, to be taken. Then, and only then, is action taken, if required.

Action? What action?

As an analogy, let us take the idea of walking into a room that is a touch cold for us. We look around for some heating. We see a radiator, turn the tap and wait for the normal physics of convection to warm the air and gradually raise the temperature in the room. If however, this time when you enter that same cold room you are in possession of a fan heater. Plug in, switch on. The blades of the fan get the air moving at speed over the heater filaments of the fan, warming it and propelling it around the room. The temperature will rise much more quickly.

That's magic, ask anyone.

I have tossed in the idea of an altered state of consciousness. What do I mean by that? We are advised that we only seem to use approximately one tenth of our brain, so, what about the other nine tenths? You're not expecting an answer are you? I don't know any more than you do. However, I have been advised that we exist on many vibrational levels within the numerous octaves of our being. The only thing being that we just neither know nor appreciate it. Many will agree that we are complex beings made up of many things. For example we are all deemed to have a mind, emotions, physical bodies, and a spiritual identity. But how many of us can say 'This is my mind'? 'This is my emotions'? 'This is my ...' whatever? They are so intermixed within us that it is practically impossible to deal with any one aspect without involving the others. It is the same within our minds. The conscious, subconscious and 'super' conscious have been named; even if not fully understood. Jung and Freud devoted their lives to working towards coming to an understanding of what the mind is all about. Not being into psychology I have no real understanding of whether or not they achieved a great deal or very little. However, such knowledge and experience as I have leads me to believe that there are, at least, the three named divisions mentioned above.

It is my understanding that once we have cleared the 'barrier' of our conscious mind we can make contact with the other levels of our mind; which we shall be dealing with in some detail a little later. It is in these other mental states that we can alter our mental perception. Many of us have spent quite a number of years Working with our minds and expanding our awareness in the endeavour to establish a mental link with these other levels of consciousness. However, we tend to blunder along since there doesn't appear to be an overall 'map' of the various 'levels' within the not-conscious mind. As an example, I eventually found myself in contact with the National Forces of my land. June initially had found herself in contact with the Dear Departed and those that Work with them. It came as quite a shock for her when I pitched up on the scene and led her into the realms that I had become aware of. We have achieved the ability to slip from one to the other now without any undue problem.

The point I am stressing is that we are all individuals and the 'map' for each person can be somewhat different until we are shown a common mind track which we can join, or not, at our discretion or leisure. However, The Merlin that I see is not, necessarily, The Merlin that June sees. Yes, we may both identify a particular symbol and associated feeling, as being allied to what we understand as The Merlin Energy, but it is always down to our individual perceptions. We do however agree as to when he is around. An indication of how these tracks may be explored will be set out later; bearing in mind that this is what worked for us and hopefully will also work for you, but you are a unique individual and it may not be exactly how you will achieve the same result. I acknowledge that our offerings are not the only way, but one of many. If after a committed, worthy attempt ours doesn't work for you, know that there is a way somewhere for you to do the same things that we do. Look at another's way and give that a try as well. One will work for you in the fullness of time.

Whilst I will be discussing a number of aspects of Working within these pages it is imperative that you concentrate on one thing at a time. When you've got that one securely under your belt, then you can move onto another phase. For example, if you are spending Monday, Wednesday and Friday on the Tarot, and then Tuesday, Thursday and Saturday you're dealing with Individual Healing, you are going to add confusion to your mind and develop neither to any great extent; not taking into account the confusion you will be engendering as your contacts line up wondering which of them is 'on call' tonight. If your Work/practice is on regular nights then your contacts will know this. If you have the personal discipline to separate them mentally it will not be a problem. Settle on one; stick with it; gain the mastery, then move on to the next if you so wish. We are back to the old adage of 'Jack of all trades, Master of none'. Having achieved your mastery don't just sit back on your

21

laurels. You can never have too much knowledge. Don't blinker your outlook. Keep your eyes and ears open. Look around and see what else you can do. You'll never know until you've had a go.

Your abilities are limitless. You are the only limitation. Your outlook will decide on what you are prepared to do or not do. There is a proverb, somewhere, that says 'Give knowledge unto a wise man and he will be yet wiser'. It's your choice. There are many things that I have explored and, finally, decided that they are not for me; but the decision comes from having made an honest investigation and reasoned the resulting answer.

Don't be put off by other people's perceptions of what you are investigating and doing. Remember, they are not you. To repeat, you are a unique individual. There has never been anyone exactly like you in the total history of the World and the Cosmos. There will never be anyone totally like you in the future. Many 'advise' us based on their own fears, anxieties and prejudices. 'I wouldn't do that if I was you.' That's just it, they're not you; so, go ahead and do it if its really what you want to do. No one can tell another what to do! The only 'Commandment', for want of a term, is that you can do anything you like as long as you hurt no-one; and that no-one includes yourself. Think about it! Life is your choice, so you choose.

From a philosophical basis, forget regrets. All of us, at sometime, look back into our past and berate ourselves over some incident or other that we did. That, in itself, is excellent. Why? When you did whatever you did at that time, you were acting on the basis of your life experience and knowledge that you held at that time. You were doing what you, in all sincerity, felt was the right thing to do for that moment in time. Perhaps a decade or more has passed since that time. You now sit back and review that time and feel that you got it all wrong. It was a 'mistake' and you should never have done it. But you did. The fact of the matter is that you are now, not only further along in your life, but you can also see that the action was not the best that you could have taken amongst the many possibilities that were open to you, even if the others were not immediately apparent at that time. We're back to the idea that when you're up to your neck in alligators it is sometimes difficult to remember that the original idea was to drain the swamp. However, the fact that you wouldn't repeat the action now is a clear indication of your growth and the accumulation of wisdom. Okay, you got it wrong then, but you wouldn't do it now. Well done, you've grown. Acknowledge your regret and then forgive it and forget it; that's it, move on. We have to move on all the time. What was true yesterday may not be so tomorrow simply because evolution drives us ever onward. Evolve or die, as the saying goes.

Which leads me to a pet hate. Take a cereal package, unopened, and stand it on one end at one end of a table. What is it doing? Not a lot, but it is in total balance. Reach out and tap the top edge of the packet so that it falls over and lays on the table. It goes out of balance and then is back in balance as it lies there. Now what is it doing? Once again, nothing; its in balance. Take hold of the packet by the end which it was initially standing upon and raise it so that the packet now stands on what was originally the top about one packet length from where it started. It is now standing back in balance, doing nothing. Repeat the process until the packet has, in turn, 'rolled' back to its previous situation of standing on its base some two packet lengths from its original position at the end of the table. What do we deduce from this? When the packet is in balance nothing happens; inertia; stagnation. How is this overcome? By an influence that causes the packet to go out of balance. In this case it was external - your hand, but it might just as well have been caused, for instance, by the contents shifting and toppling the packet. In balance, out of balance, back into balance, and so on. We started at the end of the table top and due to the imbalances occurring have moved some distance along the table.

Let's switch tack for a moment. A young babe learns to stand; it has achieved balance, but not for long. Eventually it falls over and keeps doing this until it learns to stick a foot out to catch itself. Its taken its first step. By leaning forward into an out of balance state and shooting a leg out to catch ourselves so that we get back into balance momentarily, and then repeating the process many times we walk. Movement only comes through being out of balance.

Here is the beef. A great many people are constantly demanding to be Balanced in their lives. What for? As we've just demonstrated, if something is in balance it achieves nothing through the stagnation and inertia inherent in total balance. My fervent wish is not to be in balance, because I want to move on and evolve.

Similarly we look at our lives and see all those Dark Times when Fate has thrown an, apparent, spanner in the works, but we survived and have grown through undergoing those experiences. Look also at those Bright Times when everything in the garden was golden and we sat around enjoying the luxury of the respite. Okay, we've learned the value of a respite in order to gird out loins in anticipation of the next 'problem', but, apart from that, what else have we learned in the total life experience? Not a lot! The, so called, Dark Times are the times of learning, growth and evolution, so, I suggest you look forward to the next Dark Time as a symptom of your growth and evolution and welcome it, taking the lessons you learn within yourself to add to your ever growing wisdom. It's not some Demonic Force trying to destroy you, it is simply a part of the Wonder of Life.

For those of us involved in the Western Mystery Tradition that is what everything is about. Life and yet more Life. Evolution. its not about saving up some 'goodness' in this life in order to, possibly, reap the rewards in either the hereafter or some other life. It is about existing in this world in the here and now and getting on with the things that we have to do. Thankfully, the number of insular communes where people 'drop out' of life seems to be falling. What is the point of gaining knowledge, experience, etc., and then shutting yourself away from those very people who could truly benefit from the sharing of such information? Who chooses the chosen few? Once chosen, what do they do with the information? Thankfully, more and more information is spreading out across the world as people are broadcasting their contributions to a questing humanity.

Where do these myriad quests lead us? It would appear that many, many people turn to the multifarious religions in order to find an answer for their questions. Whatever religion we look at there tends to be an inner and outer level. Back to the chosen few for the inner workings and the multitude standing, meekly, in the outer halls being told what to do or think. I am not, necessarily, saying that this is wrong. For many people this is the answer to their needs. It is, however, wrong for me. I believe, most sincerely, that we each have a right to all the information that is available 'out there'; not just selected parts of what is deemed 'good for me'. We have to acknowledge that in many instances the politics of the Quest for Power overlays the supposed Divine Law. Absolute Power corrupts absolutely. Far too many religious ideas become tainted with the interpretations of the followers in the egotistical drive for power. But, for many people there is an honest need for a religious base to live by, and I can see nothing wrong with that. There are so many religions about that I fail to see how anybody, in a lifetime, can hope to find the reality of what Truth there may be; if there is such a thing.

I fully admit that as I got my teeth into this Work I was very God(dess) orientated, Working and writing accordingly. However, as I progressed I discovered, for me, the apparent validity of a statement of Dion's in which she advised that those who are seeking a Pathway of Evolution seemed to start on a Path of Involution before finding that of Evolution. Those who are Involuting look to a Great Omnific Deity, in whatever guise, for guidance, whereas those Evolving look to the Hierarchy of the Unseen teachers for guidance.

Any Qabalist worthy of the name will spend some happy hours explaining, and demonstrating, that the same Great Omnific Deity is not the least bit interested in what you, as an individual, are doing. However, there are quite a number of 'Lesser Gods', for the want of a term, that are very much concerned in what you do. The choice, once again, is yours. Look to the Great Omnific Deity if you wish. Either pray or not as you feel fit.

To get back to the Evolution theme. Our Work is also evolving. We have only to look at the original rappings and table-tilting of the pioneer Spiritualist's in the latter part of the 19th Century and compare it with the Spiritualist activities of today. Without the dedication and efforts of the 'Greats' at the turn of this century in organisations such as the Golden Dawn and the Society of the Inner Light, I, and a lot of others like me, would be hard pressed to get on with what we are doing. They laid the framework from which we are continuing the construction, and you possibly will achieve the stars through our efforts. Not because I am any better than those who preceded me, nor that you will be better than I, but it will be the March of Evolution that carries you forward.

For instance, I am reminded of a story about Aliester Crowley. it is said that he and a man friend had themselves locked in a room overnight in order that they should summon Pan, the Goat-footed God. The next morning, when the door was unlocked, Aliester was found gibbering in a corner and the other man was dead. Aliester then spent some time in an asylum. Today I, and many others, spend quite a little time sitting communicating with Pan without any problem at all. The March of Evolution; it would appear that Aliester was jumping ahead of his time. That was his only problem.

I am also reminded of something else which invariably creates problems in the Work. Sex. In the Work that June and I do together there is sexuality, but not sex in the normal procreational manner. Wiccans will take a blade and a cup, place the two together as symbolic of the combining of the masculine and the feminine. Quite often, but not always, they may Work 'sky clad' (naked). There are many reasons for this but, in my experience of being allowed to stand with them, it has nothing to do with sex or the physical action.

I have been present and overheard various people speaking quietly to a member of the opposite sex and talking them into slipping away to 'perform a Rite to the Goddess'. The person speaking had only one thing on their mind, and it had little or nothing to do with the Goddess. She was merely an excuse for a romp.

We have found that the absence of sex quite often creates a tension between the participating members upon which the Magical Current will flow. It is my experience that the Female is the instigator of any interflow of Magical Energy. She 'calls' for the Male to give her the Energy and he responds, unreservedly, and the Energy will ride the inherent sexuality between the two of them. Physical copulation might actually decrease the flow between the two, because the sexual tension has been broken, therefore there is nothing for the Energy to flow through.

Many will counter this by stipulating that we are all a duality of the Masculine and Feminine, therefore our argument is invalid. However, whilst I agree in principle, practical experience would seem to indicate that, for the moment, it doesn't Work nearly as well, or as powerfully, as Working with a member of the opposite sex. Probably, when we have evolved a little further, this will not be the case. We must wait and see.

A few words have given us a key as to how we are progressing. Individuality, Duality, Unity. Individuality leads to Duality, which leads to Unity. We become involved in the Work of the Other Realms as Individuals. We meet another with whom we begin to Work as a Duality. This may happen many times in a lifetime until you get to the stage where two blend together and form a Magical Unity. Both June and I have spent many years Working individually in the ways that we have learnt. When we met we moved into a partnership mode and Worked together as two equals. Now in the Earth Healing mode of our Work there is little or no conversation nor questions asked between us. Each knows the other's capabilities and expertise and is confident that the Work will flow as it should. We have achieved a Unity in this mode.

Evolution is moving along. You only have to look at the many children that are being born with an increased sensitivity to things of the Other Worlds. Often quite alarming to their parents. It is nothing to be afraid of. But we do need to take time to study these matter ourselves so that we can understand what is happening to them and we can not only reassure them but also help them to come to terms with their world.

One final point before we get down to business.

Everybody is constantly demanding to be 'Aware', but, do they really understand what they are asking for? When questioned the answer invariably comes that they wish to be more aware of the Love and the Light. We all work through our Sensitivity and our Emotions. We attune these parts of ourselves in order to be more receptive to the myriad influences that are constantly flowing around and through us. That includes all those 'other' influences as well. Yes, your sensitivity does advise you of the, so called, Love and Light, but in re-tuning to such it is not, nor can it be, selective. You are heightening your ability to sense and in that sensing you are also going to come across a great deal of influences that are 'not nice'. The pain, the suffering, the emotional trauma, the hate, the despair, and all manner of things that people feel in their emotions, minds and bodies. The totality of everything that floats around us. Yes, the Love and Light are there, but so is the Dark and everything that is associated with such mental negativity. I, therefore, suggest that you either accept that you are also going to be aware of the 'problems' as well as the resolutions, or forget the whole thing.

If you've thought it over, let us get down to business.

Chapter 4

Auras & Auragraphs

Whatever we do in metaphysical terms we have to rely on our sensitivities and our awareness. Working with the auras is one of the simplest methods of developing these abilities. Whatever your aim for the future in regard to such things may be, take it slowly and steadily and prepare a solid, firm foundation upon which to build that future.

Everybody is psychic, to a greater or lesser degree. It is a natural part of our Survival Instinct and has been with us since the dawn of time. Did we dine on dinosaur, or did dinosaur dine on us? Even if, at some time, you are looking to Work in a Spiritual vein you will still need to develop the psychism as the launch pad for the Spiritual Awareness. You cannot have the latter without the former, whereas you can be psychic without being Spiritual.

A journey of a million miles starts with a single step, so, best foot forward and off we go. Let us start by looking back to school days and those, possibly, boring Science lessons and Physics in particular. I was taught that if you pass an electric current along a piece of wire a magnetic field is created around that length of wire, as shown in Diagram 1 (a). Depending upon the direction of flow, the current moves either clockwise or anticlockwise. Diagram 1 (b) shows the current coming towards you and the magnetism flowing in an anticlockwise direction, whereas Diagram 1 (c) has the current going away and the magnetism flowing in the opposite direction.

If we now turn our attention to our own physical bodies, we are told (back in boring old Biology lessons) that there are millions of nerves compactly interlaced throughout the entirety of our bodies.

Diagram 1

ELECTRO-MAGNETISM

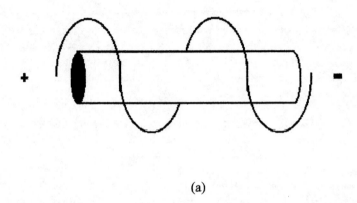

(a)

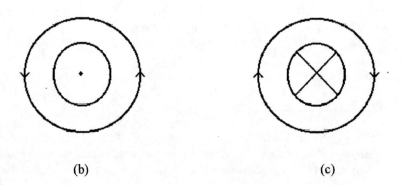

(b)   (c)

These nerves carry electrical currents conveying sensory information and are constantly active. Logic tells me that if there is a magnetic current about an electrified piece of wire, then my arm, for instance, which is carrying nervous electrical energy must also be creating a magnetic energy field about it. Therefore, the entirety of my body must be generating a similar magnetic field all about me. This electro-magnetic field is the basis of what we are now referring to when we are speaking about auras. There have been many scientific experiments since the beginning of the century which have proved the existence of the aura and many medically orientated people actually work with the auric field and find that it enhances their ability to diagnose and assist their patients.

In essence, all objects, every thing, has an aura about it. The aura of an inanimate object may be very weak and, therefore, difficult to sense, whereas anything that moves about or grows may be sensed that much easier. There are many schools of thought on how many levels of the aura there are, but for simplicity I am going to stick to a simple, basic, three that allows us to make a start and easily Work with. If the need arises for anyone to Work with the other, finer, levels then they will find them for themselves and, having found them, know what to do with them.

However, the first level of energy that we need to look at isn't a part of the aura at all, but Works so closely with it that we have to acknowledge its existence. This is the Etheric Body. It is an energy the same as the others, except that it mirrors the physical body; see Diagram 2. Many clairvoyants can see this and have often reported seeing it leave the physical body, by way of the head, shortly after death. Dr Harold Burr of Yale University, back in 1935, demonstrated that all living things are surrounded by an electro-magnetic field that organises the future development of that living organism and is a form of electrical matrix. Although it is often regarded as a part of the physical it may well be deemed as the highest level of physical matter at that point where it merges into the non-physical. The Etheric is considered to be an organised framework of lines of force, in the meshes of which the molecules of physical matter are held. It could be likened to the scaffolding, or chassis, upon which the physical body is built. It is

31

Diagram 2

AURIC REPRESENTATIONS

**Etheric Body
Mirroring the Physical**

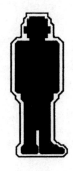

**Physical
Aura** *Every feeling physical.*

**Mental/Emotional
Aura**

Mood, thought

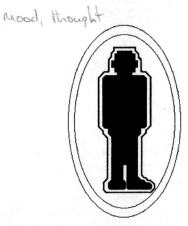

**Spiritual
Aura**

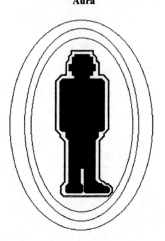

NOTE : NOT drawn to Scale

claimed that a 'life force' circulates through the Etheric, which then circulates that same 'force' to each and every cell of our body. This would suggest that the Etheric is a vehicle for transmuting vital energy into a form that can be absorbed by the physical body. This transmutation effect will be dealt with in more detail when we come to look at a method of offerring Healing to individuals. Additionally, it has been shown that the body is not the source of this energy field and therefore supposes that it continues to exist after the body has gone.

Moving on we come to the first level of the Aura, that of the Physical Body. This is the electro-magnetic field which is created, as was shown earlier, by the physical body and spreads in all directions from the body forming an almost oval shaped energy field about the individual. Some people like to describe this as an egg shape, however, my practical experience would tend to deny this. I shall leave you to discover the exact shape for yourself. This Physical aura extends on average about 4 inches from the top of the head, and about the same distance from the soles of the feet. See Diagram 2. However, depending on the physical impressions of the person it can be larger or smaller. For instance, if they are cold, the aura will be smaller, and, if they are hot, it may be a little larger. There are no hard and fast rules for its dimensions; we are back to the understanding that each and every person is a unique individual.

This aura is a reflection of what is physically happening to the physical body. Every itch, ache, twinge, tummy upset, or whatever, causes a 'tremor in the force' of this aura which can be seen by those who have developed the ability to see the auras. Not all can. I rarely do. But we can all sense the auric fields. When we do see them we quite often see these 'tremors' as bursts of colours within the aura. These colours will range from the blackest black to the whitest white and all the shades of the spectrum between. These fluctuations quite often lead some people to translate some of these colours into 'holes'. As we proposed at the beginning of this chapter, it is an electro-magnetic field. Did your Science teacher ever demonstrate a 'hole' in the magnetic field about the electrified piece of wire? Mine certainly didn't. Since both the aura and the magnetic field are forms of exactly the same process, how can there be such a thing? Given that the Aura is an electro-magnetic field, how are 'dust' and 'dirt' going to settle on it? To our minds this is all a load of bovine manure (bulls**t), usually produced by those seeking a degree of control over another person and enhancing the practitioner's prestige. It is scientifically impossible for an aura to get dirty and be in need of laundering. Come on, lets use a bit of common sense.

In regard to these colours, there are, once again, no hard and fast rules as to what each colour or shade may mean. This will only come with experience. A few 'start up' suggestions will be shown later, but they are not sacrosanct.

The next level to concern us is what we call the Mental/Emotional Aura. This exist some 8 to 12 inches from the body, 4 to 8 inches outside the Physical Aura and very similar in shape. Once again, the distance actually depends on the individual. This Mental/Emotional Aura is a reflection of every mood, and thought of the person being looked at, which is also displayed in various colours; sorry, no 'holes' either.

At many Psychic Fairs there are often people about with a modified camera selling photographs of people's auras. The Mental/Emotional Aura is what you're getting a snap-shot of, not, as is often claimed, your 'Spiritual Status' as described by your aura. You stand in front of the camera, think happy, spiritual thoughts and get a multitude of blues, greens, or violets, etc., out of the top of your head. I challenge you to go and see one of these photographers, think nasty, horrible thoughts about what a b*****d such and such is and then look at the picture. If I'm wrong, send me the photo, a truthful explanation of your thoughts at the moment the shutter went and the bill - I'll pay up and return everything to you.

Our final level is that which is referred to as the Spiritual Aura. The same shape as the others, however it can be any distance up to many yards away from the actual physical body, dependent on the individual. If someone is looking at you in a Spiritual Assessment sense, this is the level they will be looking towards; describing the colours and interpreting them in the light of the understanding of the viewer. Which doesn't necessarily mean that their vision, description and decode will automatically be correct. In regard to the Spiritual Aura, in the majority of instances, there is little need to dwell upon it too much, although it can have some uses in the longer term.

In the main we Work with either the Physical or Mental/Emotional Auras, since it can be nice to be in the same room as the edge of someone's aura. How can we sense these two auras? It is extremely helpful if you can have a 'body' upon which to exercise your skill. Preferably another person, but an animal can also be used if nobody else is available, however, recognise that a being smaller than us will have a smaller aura and you might even find that the physical aura may well be inside the fur of, say, a Burmese Cat, or show-clipped Poodle.

First of all, get the permission of your 'body' to enter their space. Have the body sat upright, relaxed, in an ordinary dining chair, or similar, with room for you to walk around them without touching them or having to climb over other furniture. (A pet asleep, or laying quietly, close by will work just as well. I am going to continue on the premise that you have a person to hand, simply adjust the movements to accommodate the animal.) Stand behind the person and raise one of your hands about three feet above the head of the body. The hand should be flat and parallel with the top of the head, fingers relaxed and comfortably open. Slowly lower your hand towards the head of the body. The hand must be 'soft' - imagine you are going to put your hand on a soap bubble and 'bounce' on the bubble without bursting it. At some point you will feel a sensation in the palm or fingers. It could be a minor change in temperature, a tingling, an itching, a pressure. No two people feel it exactly the same so I cannot be more specific. Once you feel the sensation, stop lowering your hand and get used to the feel. Bounce your hand up and down on this edge of the energy. It can be very tenuous and easily passed through, so do not worry if you miss it for the first few times. Just get your hand back to its starting position and keep raising and lowering it until you do feel that edge.

Once you are comfortable with this Mental/Emotional Aura sensation, press through that and search out the Physical Aura in exactly the same way. Bouncing your hand on that particular aura until you are comfortable with it and can recognise its touch.

Now, step back a little way and take your hand out to the side and slowly bring it in towards the body feeling both of the auras in turn. Move to the side of your 'body' and feel both the auras behind it and in front of it. Gradually move around and examine the 'shape' of the auras around the body. Now you might understand why I say its not, necessarily, egg shaped. You will find that the auras spread approximately the same distance from the physical body in all directions.

The reason we advise you to stand behind the 'body' is because you might find that your subject will actually feel you bouncing on their aura and react physically. If they can't see where your hand is at any given moment they cannot pre-empt the sensation.

You have now defined an aura and can get down to actually doing something with this knowledge. Most people say that they can't 'see' auras. Maybe not, but they can still 'sense' them. How many times have you met up with someone to whom you have taken an instant dislike? How about those whom you have met and are attracted to? You are responding, amongst other things, to entering their auric field and reacting to the emanations radiating therefrom. Someone walks up behind you and you are immediately aware that they are in a foul mood, perhaps even before you've actually seen their face or body language. You are in their auric field and responding to its vibrations.

I mentioned colours before and we can get back to them at this point. Even if you cannot 'see' the aura you can, with a little practice, time and patience, sense the colours about a person. In our workshops on Auras we get to a point in the proceedings where I sit with my back to the students, so that they cannot see my face and guess from any slight expression, and think various types of thoughts; making a note of the order I'm doing them in. Students then make a list of the colours they are perceiving and we then discuss it afterwards, whereupon I tell them what the thought was at that given point. It can get quite hilarious at times.

Get your friendly 'body' to do something similar for you. Sit about a dozen feet away and just relax and let your mental awareness advise you of the colours that are being radiated. You will soon build a personal list of colours that mean something specifically to you. The fact that one colour means something to me, may not be true for you; it could mean something entirely the opposite.

However, I am going to show a list that works for us and you can play with it as much as you like in order to arrive at your own interpretations.

Yellow	Intellect and Knowledge
Blue	Commitment, Spiritual Healing
Pink	Love, Compassion, Goodness
Red	Strength, Energy, Passion
Green	Balance, Nervous System
Grey	Depression, Anxiety, Depletion

You should note that if the colours sensed are Light the person is Progressive, if Natural, the person is Adaptable, and if Dark, the person may well be Physically or Mentally Ill.

Please remember that these colours refer to the auric emanations and should not be confused with the same colours when used in another context. Also, remember that the colours that are being perceived are a snapshot of the instant at which you are 'looking' and will probably change within minutes, if not seconds, of your perception of them.

Having arrived at your own colour combinations, what can be done with them? Whilst June is doing her Mediumship Readings she will quite often pass an Auragraph to the sitter as a further keep-sake momento of the Reading in addition to any tape-recording made. These auragraphs range over a number of designs. One shows the outline figure in the Lotus Position, another an outline figure standing with their arms by their sides, but, most often, she uses black on white line drawings of flowers. Using large boxes of coloured pencils she shades the outline with her perceived view of the Auric colours. Obviously she has to talk, at some length, on her decisions as to why certain colours have been used, which clarifies the Reading to the sitter.

Those of you that have an artistic bent can, quite easily, draw up your own flowers and shapes. The rest of us, however, can turn to photocopying line drawings the artistic ones have made, or turn to any of the many public domain Clip Art computer programs that are available and print off a master or two for photocopying.

But you have to get the groundwork done first. You have to be confident and know what you are doing. Practice, practice, practice makes permanent.

Another way to add to your perceptive ability is to Work with Psychometry. Psy what? As we stated before, every thing has an aura. Even inanimate objects. They are very, very fine and can really be on the extreme edge of anyone's perception. However, personal items, such as rings, watches, brooches and such like, if worn constantly will take an imprint of the owner wearer. It does take a bit of time for this to happen, but it will do eventually.

For some reason unknown to me it appears that Gold is the best medium with which to work. It takes and holds the imprint much stronger than many other substances. It seems that in days of old, long before knights were bold, people were a lot less acquisitive and all their 'wealth' was carried or worn about their person. Naturally, any gold they possessed was also worn. This held a very strong image of the mind and personality of the owner. Battles were sometimes fought in order for one King to take the gold of another King. The victorious King, through his, or a servant's, sensitivity could now 'tune in' to the vanquished King and sense how this other King would react etc.. He now had far more control over the deposed monarch. It follows, therefore, that all the gold in Fort Knox and the Bank of England and elsewhere is, in fact, valueless inasmuch as it holds no imprint of the owner, therefore there is no control over anybody.

Back to work. Borrow an object from an acquaintance, not a friend, and hold it lightly in the palm of your hand and sense the electro-magnetic field that is now surrounding the object. Tell it as it is. It doesn't matter how stupid or silly it may seem to you, the sensations you are picking up may well have some deep significance to the owner. Why not a friend? Quite simply because, as a friend, you will obviously know them quite well through your friendship and this knowledge may well colour your perceptions of the sensations you are receiving. Your mind will get in the way; it always does.

As Dion Fortune once said of the Qabalah, it is about training the Mind, not informing it. These simple methods of Working with the Auras are about strengthening and training your sensitivities.

Chapter 5

Protection

We come to a very thorny subject. June has been a Medium since birth and at two years of age was playing with 'unseen' children. She had no idea of what protection was, nor of the need for it. I had come upon the metaphysical scene in the 1960s by way of a Spiritualists' Church where I was taught to 'wrap a cloak of protection' about me and to pray to the Almighty for my protection whilst I was Working Spiritually. I did it. Having left the Fraternity of the Inner Light I was Working with The Merlin Energy and utilising the Lesser Pentagram Banishing Ritual whenever I sat to make contact. (This rite is described later.) It was really great to have those Pentagrams flaming around me. One evening I had sat as normal, set the metaphysical Pentagrams blazing and had called on The Merlin to see if there was any information to be passed to me. Apparently there wasn't, because there was no sign of The Merlin anywhere around. I had stood up, extinguished the flames and then sat to write up a non-event report in my Diary. As I had put the final full stop at the end of my report I had become aware of The Merlin close by my left shoulder. I won't use his actual words (blunt Anglo-Saxon), but the general gist was to stop being an idiot and wasting time and energy with such things as they were totally unnecessary. I freely admit I was not a happy lad when he departed without any further explanation. However, somewhat tremulously I acceded to the wish and have never used that, nor any other, form of protection since.

Both June and I have the supreme protection; our minds. We have broken the Establishment bred fear and boldly go where we will. In our joint experience, which covers some eighty odd years, we have discovered that the Satanic Dark does not exist except in the Mind of Man. There are a vast number of Energies and Forces 'out there', but, we are impressed that not one of them may so much as harm a single hair on any of our heads. Yes, 'things' do happen, but it is our interpretation of our perceptions that decides it is a 'nasty'.

For instance, you have altered your state of consciousness and the vision arises of being deep in the desert in the middle of the night. There is only starlight since there is no moon. Through the gloom you begin to make out a tall figure stood in front of you. It is totally covered in black and you can see no face. What do you do? You are under the impression that you have two alternatives. Flight or fight. You break the connection and find yourself sitting in a muck sweat back in your chair. Escaped! Alternatively, you hurl thunder-bolts of Light at it, whereupon it disappears and you come back with a sense of having 'overcome the Dark'; feeling very proud of yourself.

But there was another alternative. You could have tried a simple, polite, hello. Whereupon the figure would have turned in the darkness to face you and you would have seen a Bedouin; a desert nomad. I am led to believe that they wear dark clothing at night in the knowledge that such insulates them from the biting chill. They would have been prepared to talk with you of the ways of the desert, the movements of the sands, the creatures that live there and shown you some of the secrets of the stars of the sky.

Flight, fight or polite? I have always found that courtesy opens every door; which doesn't mean grovelling on hands and knees. They are our equals and need us more than we need them.

Throughout the world there are millions and millions of people who have little or no interest in the Other Worlds and they still live honest, deeply fulfilled lives. In comparison those of us that do have such an interest and are prepared to Work towards a greater level of communication number a lot, lot less. The Management need those few and, therefore, will not allow any harm to come in that manner. That does not mean to say that we are all going to live on Easy Street. Far from it. If anything we are going to be pitched into all sorts of turmoil to give us the ability to do even more on their behalf. It is like any sword blade. The metal is placed in the fire, beaten on the anvil and plunged into the icy cold waters, time and time again. Without this tempering process the blade would shatter on its first impact. So it is with us. As we become more and more aware of what is around us, so we become receptacles for more and more energies to Work with.

I repeat, it is not the Dark Satanic Forces ranging themselves in battle order to steal our souls and take us to damnation. There are, however, I have been told, certain Forces whose role it is to 'slow us down' and stop us from over-running ourselves and falling by the wayside. Acting like brakes on the wheels of evolution to keep things moving at the correct pace.

The Christian Concept of the Devil was a device manufactured by the early Church Fathers in order to instil their will upon the peasants and keep them in line. It was a part of that gross materialism process I spoke of earlier. Ruling by Fear. "You will work for me or I'll whip you", so you worked. "You will worship God in the manner I prescribe, or else you will spend eternity in hell fire", so you worshipped as you were told. "Go to sleep, or the bogey man will get you" so we turn over and, hopefully, go to sleep. Rule by Fear.

Hopefully it is coming to an end, but the constructed 'thought forms' of the Devil, demons and such like still persist. Many people believe in the Devil, therefore, to them, the Devil exists and still has a part to play in their lives. But, it is not an Energy in the sense that the others are. The Devil only exists in the minds of those who wish to remember him - a created thought form.

I do not deny the power of the mind in this context and treat it with respect; even if the idea is not for me. Everyone has the right to believe in whatever they wish to believe in and I will stoutly defend their right to do so. I also recognise that there are many people who still have yet to break free from such things, but I know that, eventually they will. In the meantime I offer some ideas on basic protection which will be of help to anyone who feels the need.

The first is the simple prayer. Have a chat with your concept of the Almighty. There is no need to go into ritualistic repetition unless you feel that 'Hail Mary' or 'Our Father ...' makes you feel more at ease. Talk as if you are talking to a friend who is listening to what you are saying and taking notice.

Many people are convinced that they are picking up 'negative vibes' from other people; even being under psychic attack from someone else. I insist that no-one can 'attack' you unless you want them to. However, if you are not yet ready to put that to the test, here is a method of 'shielding' yourself from such a person. We have spoken in some depth about the Auras and it is through these that we construct a psychic shield. For the sake of argument, let us assume that the person in the next office to you is 'having a go' at you. All you do is visualise a 'mirror' on the outer edge of your Mental/Emotional Aura in the direction of that person, which will reflect such thoughts or feelings back to the originator. In this instance, only do it in the one direction.

You walk into a room full of people, all of whom appear to be radiating animosity towards you. From a level slightly above the top of your head, down to a level just under your feet, 'silver' the Mental/Emotional Aura to reflect those feelings back to the other people. Never, never, 'silver' the totality of your Mental/Emotional Aura. Always leave at least two directions open, even if they are only above and below. There are a lot of Energies that free float in our atmosphere which we really need as a part of our overall well-being; you cannot afford to shut those out as well.

Having felt the beneficial effect of this exercise, you can then turn their animosity to your advantage. On the outer edge of your Mental/Emotional Aura you can visualise a 'Transmutation Screen'. This is a colourless skin that absorbs all the vibrations that are apparently heading your way and turns the 'negative' energies into 'positive' ones. You can 'tune' this to allow the other free flowing energies to enter without hindrance and keep yourself naturally 'topped up' with them. Devils heading your way, pass through this skin and arrive at you as angels. The ordinary 'positive' energies pass through unaffected.

You can also put a 'shield' around your home and family, if you wish. Work out the rough physical centre of your home space, which includes any garden and other buildings such as sheds or garages. Concentrate on this centre point and visualise the 'Transmutation Screen' about the size of a small cup on the ground at this point. Gently expand it so that it passes through everything between the centre and the limits of your home space until it sits like an igloo style dome over the whole property, high enough to cover the entirety of the roof of your house. But your property is neither round nor a true square style shape? This doesn't matter. No one says that it has to have a perfect circular base. There can be any odd angles and shapes to fit what is yours. You could even end up with a cubic shape; especially if you live in a mid-floor apartment or flat. You must never ever allow your 'shield' to enter anyone else's 'space'. Repeat this exercise daily until the 'dome' becomes a 'reality' in your mind; it exists and Works to protect the home base. If your garage, or something similar, is away from your property, you repeat the whole process at that site as well.

Okay, our base is now a 'fortress'. What about the immediate family? I stress that word 'immediate'. Only your spouse or partner and any children of either of you. They are your responsibility. No one else. You would be interfering with another's life, which shouldn't happen. However, as far as this immediate family is concerned they need not know what you have done, or are doing. There are a large number of couples where one member is totally against any thought or dealings in the metaphysical and to advise them that 'magic' was being used to protect them would create disharmony in the relationship.

A materialist in the partnership can be a tremendous bonus in any Working. For instance, you have been in an altered state of consciousness and received some wonderful input. You come back to this world and wander around; bubbling with excitement, still enamoured of the occasion. You meet up with your partner and, possibly, share the occasion with them. If they are supportive they will be happy for you, but might point out that whilst it must have been a marvellous experience for you, there is the small problem of the electric bill that has arrived and needs paying, but there is a shortfall in the cash-flow. Bump, you're back in this world and you settle down to dealing with the physical problems. A very real experience that puts things into a true perspective.

Back to protecting your family. You spend some time watching your family coming and going from home. As you see them pass through the 'screen' you visualise a blister breaking free of the 'dome' and forming a bubble about your family member, which accompanies them everywhere that they go. As they return to the home and pass back inside, the personal bubble is absorbed by the home 'screen'. Going out in the car? As it, too, passes through the 'screen', so that blister forms a bubble about the entire car, being absorbed back into the 'dome' upon its return. Whatever you do, don't get the idea that the family or car becomes invulnerable. They certainly don't. Normal road and personal safety factors still apply. Travel with safety in mind, no matter how secure you may feel with the other worlds.

There is a little Wiccan/Pagan Invocation that we sometimes use which brings a sense of calmness to any travels that we undertake.

> *"May the God of Going go with us; let us not be involved in, nor the cause of, any accident."*

A polite *'thank you'* when the journey is over does no harm and could pay dividends in the longer term. Who knows?

As your Working ability increases you might feel the need for something with a little more impact, that is where the Pentagrams come in.

The Lesser Pentagram Banishing Ritual

This Exercise sets up a secure, sacred space in which to Work and make contact with the other realms. It requires to be completed at the start of each period of Working and then dispersed at the end of that same period. It is imperative that you do disperse it, otherwise you could find yourself somewhat out of sorts with the physical reality around you. It is extremely potent and should be treated with the greatest respect.

Physically stand facing the East, hands by your side with the palms facing forwards. State, aloud or mentally, "*Above my head is the Kingdom, the Power and the Glory, for ever and ever, Amen*".

Extend the index and middle fingers of your right hand to act as a pointer. Bring your hand across the body to a point just in front of your left hip. With your arm straight draw a visualised straight line of blue fire to the limit of your arm above your head, pause, then draw another line down to the level of your right hip. Pause again, then draw a further line across to the level of your left shoulder. Another pause, then move your arm across your body in a straight line to the level of your right shoulder. A final pause, then draw the final line of the pentagram (a five pointed star) from your right shoulder back to your left hip.

Let your arm drop back to your side and pause for a moment or two whilst you firm up the visualised pentagram in your mind's eye.

Then stab your two fingers into the centre of the pentagram, stating "*In the name of Adonai (R-don-I), I open the East.*"

With your arm still extended, turn to your right to face the South, drawing an arc of fire as you go.

Drop your arm and repeat the whole process again. Left hip, over head, right hip, left shoulder, right shoulder, left hip. Stab the centre, repeating the same words, except it is now the South you are opening.

With your arm still extended, turn to your right to face the West, drawing an arc of fire as you go.

Drop your arm and repeat the whole process again. Left hip, over head, right hip, left shoulder, right shoulder, left hip. Stab the centre, repeating the same words, but now the West.

With your arm still extended, turn to your right to face the North, drawing an arc of fire as you go.

Drop your arm and repeat the whole process again. Left hip, over head, right hip, left shoulder, right shoulder, left hip. Stab the centre, repeating the same words to open the North.

With your arm still extended, turn to your right to face the East again, connecting the final arc of fire.

You are now surrounded by a circle of fire with four flaming pentagrams at the cardinal points.

Stand in the centre of your circle, raise your arms from your sides to shoulder height, palms forward and state, whilst visualising the Archangelic forms that are facing you in a way that you understand, "*In the East, Raphael; in the West Gabriel; in the South Michael (Mik - i - el); in the North Uriel. About me flame the Pentagrams, behind me shines the Six-rayed Star. Above my head is the Glory of God in whose hands is the Kingdom, the Power and the Glory, for ever and ever, Amen*".

As you become more and more accomplished at this, you can carry out the whole Exercise in the imagination.

The phrase about the Six-rayed Star is one of aspiration.

The Closing is almost the same, except that you start facing the East, turning to your left to erase the arc of fire that leads to the North, then erase the pentagram by drawing it backwards. Left hip to right shoulder, to left shoulder, to right hip, to above the head and back to the left hip.

Fingers again in the centre of where the pentagram had been, you turn to your left, erasing that arc leading to the West.

Erase that pentagram, erase the arc to the South, erase that pentagram, erase the arc to the East, erase that pentagram.

With everything now 'switched off', stand in the centre of where your circle had been and raise your arms to shoulder height and repeat the complete earlier statement about the Archangels, except that at this point you visualise them facing away from you.

As I said, it is very potent and must be treated with the greatest respect. If you open with it, you must close with it as well.

Chapter 6

Making Contact

We have arrived at a situation where you should have a Working knowledge of the Auras about you and how, if necessary, you can protect yourself. We move on to developing a contact with the Other Realms; entering an altered state of consciousness. The other realms are hard to describe without going into great philosophical treatise, but I'll try to keep things as simple as possible. Spiritualism advises us that we are all spirit incarnate and that when we die the spirit is released from the physical body and travels in another dimension, where it continues to grow and evolve. It could be argued, therefore, that although the spirit is within each of us, it also exists in that spiritual domain whilst we are living a physical life, making each of us a two dimensional being. The mind is said to also exist alongside the spirit, but at a slightly different vibrational rate, extremely close to that spirit, practically inseparable. The mind has the ability to also make that simple, yet quantum leap, from its physical environment to the mental level of another vibration. Hence the mind is also two dimensional. Two dimensions and two dimensions makes us multi-dimensional.

The other dimensional realms are best experienced rather than taught or explained. However, let us take a simple analogy on how the various contacts can be made. Visualise your Mind as a simple radio set; the type many of us have in our homes. On the dial there is an indication of a number of different wave-bands. Short Wave 2 (SW2); Short Wave 1 (SW1); Long Wave (LW); Medium Wave (AM or MW); Frequency Modulation (FM). In the normal course of events we should be living with our radio either switched off or on very, very low. When we get into a Contact situation we turn the radio on or up. Depending on what we are

Diagram 3

CONTACT LINKS

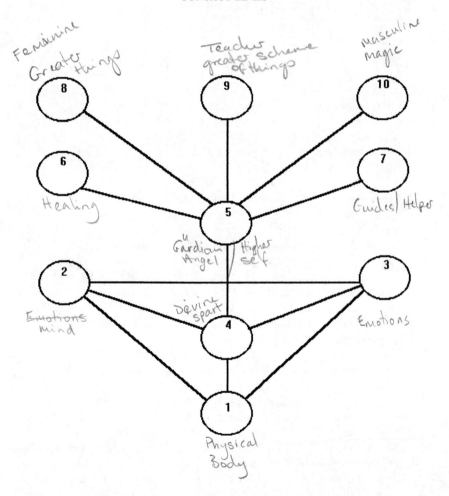

50

doing we go to the appropriate wave-band. For instance, and only as a suggestion, let us assume that SW2 is the wave-band for Self Awareness; SW1 is the wave-band for Psychism; AM (MW) is the level of Mediumship; LW is the band for Healing; FM is the wave-band for Other Things. When you settle yourself down, so you adjust your particular radio wave-band.

Tightening things down a little more, no one is any position to fully describe how we make these contacts, they just seem to happen when you put yourself in the appropriate situation. However, The Merlin suggested the idea of the following explanations as possible examples of how things work. I refer you to Diagram 3 which is a 'map' of the objective links.

Let us accept that you have a Physical Body (1) - if not we have a serious problem with what we are doing. Also, you have a Mind (2) and your Emotions (3). This triangle would seem to be the basis of your individuality as a person.

However, at (4) we have what is often termed the Spirit Within, the Divine Spark, which can link with the other three attributes of yourself. In order to establish a contact with that Divine Spark you need to get your body comfortable and relaxed, calm the emotions and quieten the mind (you can never switch theses two off completely, but you can control them). To my mind, when people talk about centring themselves, this is what I believe they should be endeavouring to do. The Divine Spark will respond to this silence and begin to communicate with either the Mind or the Emotions. In the beginning it may seem to just be a load of garbage that you are finding coming into your mind, but, with practice you suddenly find that the link is strengthening and very personal information will be forthcoming.

Once you have assimilated these facts about yourself the link to (5) begins to be forged. What is this point? Once again, there are many names for this, amongst which are Guardian Angel, Doorkeeper, Super Consciousness, Higher Self, and many more. A rose by any name smells just as sweet. In effect the concept of the Guardian Angel may well be the nearest correct name by virtue of its activities. This point is the filter through which everything

51

from the Other Realms is strained. The Guardian Angel is in a position to 'see' what you are doing and allow the appropriate link to be formed from the other 'points' that lie beyond it.

For instance, if you are seen to be in a Healing situation, whether it be from a Physical or Mental/Emotional perspective, the Guardian Angel will open the link to point (6) which is the area of the Spiritual Healers; discarnate entities who have an interest in things Medical. From them will come a very subtle energy that will be passed through the Guardian Angel (5) to the Divine Spark (4) which will then pass it to the Emotions (3) and then to the Physical Body (1) for transmission to the patient. We will deal with this in greater detail in the next Chapter.

However, should you be in a position where information or guidance is required the Guardian Angel will open the link to point (7) where those who are often known as Guides and Helpers reside. Discarnate beings who have set themselves to being available to help those in incarnation who seek information about themselves and the way their lives are progressing. The information is passed from the Guides (7) to the Guardian Angel (5), to the Divine Spark (4), through to the Mind (2) and then to the Physical (1) for the words to be spoken. The information that is passed will never include anything which will cause physical, mental or emotional harm to any other person. Certain serial killers have always claimed that the 'voices' told them to kill. That is as maybe, but based on our experience we have never been in contact with anyone, or any thing, who has told us to strike out at another person. It is against all the 'rules' of contact. They just cannot, and will not, suggest such a thing. In the highly unlikely event that you should find yourself in this position, back out and run a check on your linkages and most especially your own motives in such a case.

Up to this point all those who have been contacted are interested in individuals and their immediate families. How their lives are progressing and how they are learning from the life experiences. They have no authority to tell anyone how to live their lives nor to interfere. They are simply allowed to offer advice, which may be taken or ignored by the recipient. They are not Fortune Tellers either. If you are concerned about whether you should keep you current job or search for another one; sell your house; run off with the person down the road; or any other similar decision, don't bother asking these Guides, because they will not tell you. These are decisions that you have to make and stand or fall by those decisions. Whatever information you will receive may well, quite often, be in symbols or riddles and it is down to you to unravel them.

Beyond this point we move into the areas of those who have no real interest in you as an individual, other than that you are involved with the Work; whatever that may be for you as a unique person. They are involved in far greater things; such as the evolution of Planet Earth and all that have an existence within that sphere. For information as to whatever requirements are needed for the situation that you are involved with, the Guardian Angel (5) will establish the link with the Feminine Principle of the Area of concern (8), pass the information to the Divine Spark (4), which will then appropriately split the input to the points of the Mind (2) and the Emotions (3), for assimilation within the Physical (1).

Should you be in the position of requiring Energy to carry through some form of 'Magical' Working, then the Guardian Angel (5) will establish the link with the Masculine Principle of the Area of concern (10) which will generate that which is needful, pass it to the Guardian Angel (5), which will then pass it to the Divine Spark (4) and through, direct, to the Physical (1) for transmission.

On those occasions that you are seeking the Philosophy to explain what is really going on in the greater scheme of things, the Guardian Angel will establish a link with the Teachers, for want of a term, at (9). The information, once again, is passed to the Guardian Angel (5), to the Divine Spark (4) and thence, in the main, to the Mind (2), although the Emotions (3) do get some input in certain circumstances.

Now, although our diagram may suggest that there is some distance between the physical (1) and, say, (10), I am advised that the actual measurement is less than the thickness of a molecule.

From a subjective view point, however, we need to look once more at our old Biology lessons. I was taught that in order to see anything, the light is taken in through the eye where it impinges on the rods and cones at the back of the eye, which produces a chemical reaction, which, in turn, creates electrical pulses that are fed along the nerves to the visual centre of the brain to be interpreted into colours and pictures. The image lasts for something like one twentieth of a second and is then renewed. Similarly when we hear something the sound is perceived within the inner ear and also turned into electrical impulses that travel along the auditory nerves to the aural centre of the brain for interpretation. If anything comes into contact with our skin, millions of nerve ends react and trigger electrical impulses along the nerves to our sensory centre of the brain to be decoded.

The beings that we are making contact with exist as energy forms, vibrating on a different frequency to ourselves. Their vibratory rate is so much faster than ours that our normal senses cannot perceive them. So, what happens? These beings, as we have said, are best described as pure energy and as such can do certain things that our gross materialism cannot, but they can radiate their energy into our dimension in order to cause certain things to happen. In the metaphysical there are three main methods of perceiving other things. Clairvoyance, clear seeing; clairaudience, clear hearing and clairsentience, clear sensing or feeling. The being contacted creates electrical 'interference' to the nerves that run to the various centres of the brain, which causes the appropriate centre to interpret the impulses as pictures, sounds or feelings. The physical eye, ear or whatever plays no part in the perception.

Hopefully you now have a general idea of how things may be Working, so, lets get down to it. There follows a number of suggestions that you may find helpful. Whilst I'll refer to them as 'rules', they aren't, and I use the word simply for the sake of brevity in later pages. In order to obtain the best results it is recommended that you get into a comfortable position, but not lying down (this could lead to you falling asleep), and try to ensure that you will not be disturbed. Telephone off the hook? Animals out of the room? No visitors expected? Electrical appliances switched off? You wont want a meal to spoil whilst you are busy - only the old Gods needed burnt offerings.

Make sure that the environment where you are going to Work is at a comfortable temperature and that you are not sitting in draught. There is absolutely no need to be uncomfortable, nor to practice any of the 'mystical postures'. However, if you are comfortable with your left toe up your right nostril, do it. Comfort is the key. Some may find that the lighting of an incense stick is beneficial, but it is not essential. I would suggest something light and fairly delicate, such as a gentle sandalwood, if you feel it is really necessary.

Many maintain that you should 'sit' at a specific time of the day each day. However, I feel that, under the present pressures and stresses of life in general, this is no longer totally practicable. Make sure you do it at the most convenient time for you on a particular day. This can often involve an element of 'forward planning'. If you are going out for a meal, to a dance, disco, whatever, sit quietly before you go since you may not be in a fit state upon your return. Alcohol and/or a heavy meal tends to remove the essential mind control you need.

I am a firm believer in sitting for 5 minutes a day for 5 days and then taking two days off, rather than sitting for 25 minutes once a week. You need a couple of regular days off to give yourself a break and give yourself a chance to assimilate whatever may be happening to you as a result of your making the linkages. You need time to adjust to the new awareness and the knowledge of your 'new' abilities. Be gentle on yourself.

Be warned that once you start there may well be a quickening of your Life in general. Lots of little irritations will arise that must be resolved, their lessons learnt, and new understandings of life experienced. It is not, as many have claimed in the past, the other realms testing you, trying to deflect you from this path. It is a clearing of the base metal of the essential you. A tempering of the blade to make it strong and useable. A clearing of aspects of your life that must be cleansed before you can Work. Face up to them, learn from them and emulate the phoenix; arise and fly free from the ashes. In preparation, do whatever you feel will be conducive to attaining a relaxed state of mind and body. Try releasing those tight constrictions in your clothing, be comfortable.

Rest assured that you are about to take part in something very worthwhile. There is nothing to be afraid of except yourself and your own personal fears. It is not my habit to ask anyone to do anything that I haven't already done myself. I am not into pain on any level. I don't like it. By persuasion I am a devout coward.

Above all, take your time; there is no need to rush. Softly, softly ...

So what do you do? Basically, nothing.

As we said before, sit comfortably, calm the emotions and quieten the mind. By all means, if you feel the need, do a meditation as a method calming yourself down. However, once you are calm, don't meditate, contemplate, or any other 'ate'. If you are meditating, for instance, your mind is occupied with following a defined pathway; for example, on path, follow path, come to gate, open gate, go through gate, close gate, follow path, and so on. You're mind is busy so how can anything else get in to communicate with you?

The first few things that may begin to filter in could well seem like a load of rubbish, however, bear with it, and you will soon find that 'proper' information will begin to come through. The question immediately rises as to the source of this information. Is it yourself, your own mind or ego, or is it the Spirit Within? When you are actually sitting in order to make the contact accept that it is not yourself, nor your ego; it is coming in by way of your Guardian Angel. Just for the few minutes that the sitting is going, it is them. Watch and see; look at the information you are receiving and see if it proves to be viable.

Now, what do you do with this information? You write it down. You need to keep an accurate record of all of your input because you may not see the fulfilment of the information for some weeks, months, or even years. I keep a diary of everything seen, heard or sensed, plus any 'sittings' that we do are tape-recorded and then transcribed, but the latter is going to extremes. You need not go that far at this stage.

You are in the process of making contact with yourself. Finding out about yourself, who you are, what you are and what makes you tick. Written over the Ancient Gateway of the Temples of the Mysteries are two words : Know Thyself. That is what you are doing in this initial process. Once you have accepted yourself, warts and all, the 'Guardian Angel' will kick itself into gear and begin to make the other links available.

We hit a problem. The material can come as patches of colour or symbols. The problem lies in the decode. Various colours can have individual meanings for each of us. For instance, for me, Red shows when energy is on the move; Blue can show when healing energy is about; Green can show things need calming down, and so on. But, it is down to you to come to understand what each colour means for you.

Similarly, the same has to be said for any symbols that appear. A New Moon means one thing for me, another for June and, probably, another for you. It is up to you to say to your contacts that you don't understand what a particular symbol means and wait for them to clarify their intent. You have to create your own Dictionary of Symbols. The many published Dictionaries that I have obtained over the years have only led me into deeper confusion. This is something very personal and intimate for you, the unique individual.

Okay, so you're beginning to get these thoughts or pictures trickle into your mind and you are keeping your diary. What is happening? There are many levels of contact. This is the first, and is referred to as 'Inspiration'. Thoughts rising from somewhere; the Divine Spark, the Guardian Angel, or elsewhere. The other levels of 'Control' and 'Trance' are specialised activities requiring different circumstances and will not be dealt with in these pages other than advising that they exist. 'Control' is where the person is partially conscious and the entity or being exerts a greater influence and controls the person's thoughts and, sometimes, actions. 'Trance', on the other hand, is where the being or entity is

57

able to use the voice and memory of the sitter because the sitter is totally unconscious and has no knowledge of any of the activities that are carried out whilst entranced.

I do not recommend that you get involved in these aspects, until you have forged very strong, secure links with all the other aspects that are available to you and fully understand what is going on. Stick with the inspirational input and Work with yourself and get those links fully on line. Do not, however, make any decisions on what you think you will be doing with these things in the future. Once you have made such a decision you are imposing limitations on yourself. There is an old adage that you should sit and write down a list of all the things you want to do. At the same time you should also make a list of all the things you don't want to do. Take the list of those things you do want to do and throw it away, because you'll be doing everything that is on the other list.

As we have said, there is no rush in this self preparation. If you take three paces forwards and then drop back two, you are still one pace further forward than you were before. It takes time and personal training. Only you can achieve anything and it doesn't matter if it takes a month, a year or a decade. You will get there in the end if you persist. You might even find that in the normal course of life you will be Working on those links when you least suspect it; finding yourself repeating some received information to a friend when they come to you to talk or for help, or even finding that the Healing Energies are flowing from you to someone who is unwell.

The Guardian Angel is indicating that he, she or it (shimit? Sh(e), (Hi)m, It) is keeping a very close eye on you and using your natural abilities already, even if you aren't yet fully on line.

A warning. When the contact is well established you will find that 'they' are so pleased that you have made it and they will chatter away, hour after hour, if you let them. Don't. Establish some discipline, both for yourself and for them upstairs. Stipulate that you will be available at a suitable date, time, place, and beyond that, tell them to keep away. Imagine you are in the supermarket,

58

wheeling your trolley around the aisles. Suddenly, 'someone' turns up and 'sits' on your shoulder. They tell you that the lady further along the aisle, the one in the red coat, is their daughter, and they ask you to go and tell her that Mum is now fit and well and that she is happy where she is. Unless you can run a lot faster than a flying can of beans, don't. Her daughter may not want to know.

You must stay in control at all times, and Work when you want to Work, and not outside then.

One other thing. Remember that I keep going on about you being in control of what is happening to you? Without going into any depth, let us categorically say that the use of any form of drug to enhance your perceptions is totally out. The higher energies barely tolerate the use of commercial tobacco in cigarettes and such and are adamant that anything stronger is totally out of the question. How can you be in control of yourself if you're under the influence of either alcohol or drugs? Alcoholic drinks? All things in moderation, but not when you are preparing to Work. A little wine soothes the belly.

As things progress you may well find that you are receiving information from the deceased. Relatives and friends who have passed on. It is nothing to be alarmed at as it is quite, quite natural. It is an indication, if nothing else, that your links are becoming stronger and stronger. The Guides are in contact with the realms of the deceased and they allow your relatives to step forward and Work through the Guide's energy to pass proof of their survival beyond physical death. You have to bear in mind, however, that if Great Aunt Freda was a pain in the butt she still will be. No matter what instant enlightenment she may have received in the transition if she returned as an enlightened being you probably wouldn't recognise her, so she has to come back to you as you would remember her; a pain in the butt. Don't get over enamoured of the Guides or the deceased; you don't need to get into Ancestor or Guide Worship. Do not expect your Great Aunt Freda to turn up every time you sit quietly. There is the Biblical myth that when we go to heaven we spend eternity sitting on a cloud, going plunk, plunk on a harp, yodelling hosanna forever. Afraid not. Whilst we can have no real comprehension of what they actually do, they are busy with whatever it is. When you are sitting it is more than possible that Great Aunt Freda is 'on shift' doing whatever it is she is charged with doing and cannot, at that time, get away to gossip nostalgically with you. Perhaps another relative may, or may not, turn up. You are very much in their hands as to who is available at that time.

From various conversations with our contacts we have come to the conclusion that we each create our own heaven or hell. When we pass over we go to the region that we expect to go to. Our mind has already decided what the next world shall be for us. If we expect to find ourselves on a cloud with wings, harp and a halo, then that is what we'll find. If we expect hell fire and damnation, complete with a tail, horns and a pitchfork, then that also. If we expect to sleep until the Trump of Doom, then so be it - at least until we get fed up with it and wake ourselves up to go have a look around. So, don't be overly surprised if you expect some particular friend to pop back to have a chat and they don't appear for some time. As suggested earlier, they could be extremely busy, or in some other place doing whatever they expect to be doing when they pass over.

In regard to the Guides, cast your mind back to your first year at school. You had a teacher who taught you what you needed to know at that time, but as you moved on through the various years so your teachers changed and taught you different things. It is the same with the Guides. The fact that a particular Guide was with you last week has no relevance; you may well have grown during those seven days and you now have a Guide who will be able to assist you in the next stage of your growth.

A further thought to be borne in mind is that you are, and must be, as I have repeatedly maintained, in control of you and what is going on. If you feel you are shaking with an excess of energy, for instance, tell 'upstairs' to back off. You have to be comfortable at all times. Any physically reactive impressions have to be within your normal bodily tolerances. We hear of many weird tales of people rolling and sliding around on the floor because the spirit of an alligator or snake has entered their bodies. What a load of rubbish! It is merely the obsession of the individual. No other

60

Being can enter your body; its metaphysically impossible. Admittedly they can come extremely close, penetrating your aura and promoting the sensations of size, shape and colour, but they cannot take over your body. They cannot possess your body. Many so called cases of possession are in fact an obsession by the person concerned. They lead such mundane lives, they become obsessed with the idea of Napoleon, Josephine, Queen Victoria, Abe Lincoln, or any other more interesting personage and decide that their lives would be more fun than their own. Obsession, not possession.

A final thought on making the initial contact; expect nothing, accept everything. Write it down; make it a physical reality; check, check and double check all input.

Chapter 7

Healing People

Once you've made your start by doing a regular, committed sit and are tuning in to the Inner Self and your Guardian Angel you should find that it won't be long before you will recognise, in your own way, that things are beginning to happen. Most noticeable amongst these may well be a sensation of heat, cold or tingling in either, or both, hands or feet. Simple little indications that a form of power is passing through you. If it is hitting your feet it is passing straight through and into the Earth; which is brilliant, but you wont be able to appreciate it for a century or two - perhaps in the life after the next life; if you are into Reincarnation. If the feet are humming away, it only takes a simple thought for you to redirect it to your hands. Think hands, not feet, and it will be so. So, your hands are singing away, now what do you do? Put them on the Earth again to 'earth' or 'ground' the energy whilst you make arrangements for your friendly 'body' to come back on the scene; the person who let you feel their auras whilst you were checking that chapter out.

You are going to be investigating 'hands on healing'. This term is very misleading because the very last thing you should ever do is touch your patient's body. We are looking for potential 'healers' not 'feelers'. You are going to be working on their auras again. The Physical and the Mental/Emotional Auras.

Get them to sit in the chair again and relax whilst you put your hands on their Physical Aura. Slide your hands over the outer 'skin' of this aura and you should feel small areas of different temperatures in the 'skin' of the aura. Even if your 'patient' is 100% fit and healthy, certain natural bodily functions will stimulate a response on the aura. For instance, if your 'patient' is a female and menstruating there may well be activity in the region of the lower stomach creating a temperature change. Similarly, if they have not long finished eating a meal their gastric juices will be doing their stuff in the abdominal area, thereby stimulating a response in the Physical Aura. Let your hands move over the aura and seek out the temperature variations, getting used to finding them. Whilst you are doing this you should begin to practice the most important rule of Healing. Keep your mouth shut. Say nothing at what you are finding.

Having found two hot or cold spots, step back and take a minute or two to calm your mind and emotions, centre on the Divine Spark, and ask for some guidance. You will feel the humming begin or intensify so step forward and place your hands on the two spots you found before. Don't be concerned if you have to slide around a bit to get back on them, that's okay, just so long as you get to them in the end. To all intents and purposes you could well go to sleep or read a book now. There is nothing else for you to do other than stand there and let the energy pour through you. In the UK we look on ourselves as drain-pipes through which the power flows, but I understand that some Native Americans refer to the process as 'hollow bones', which is a lot more poetic. However, the resulting effect will be the same.

You will know when the process is complete when you find that either the temperature differential disappears or your hands stop fizzing. Slide on around the rest of the aura to see if there are any other spots that need attention. If there are, repeat the same process as before. If there aren't, drop your hands, stand back from your patient and silently say a polite thank-you. Step further aside and keep a close eye on your patient. It is quite possible that they may well have drifted off into a doze, or even a heavy sleep, whilst you have been Working on them. You don't want them to fall off the chair and break something like the vase, goldfish bowl or an arm. Don't hurry them, let them come back at their own pace and begin to move when they are ready. By all means chat with them after you have finished. Did they feel anything? Heat, coldness, tingling, nothing? All of these answers are perfectly acceptable.

Unlike drugs, and cooking time, you cannot overdo it. Your patient will not go on overload, over-dose, nor be over-cooked. You cannot feed in too much healing energy. However do not get the idea that you are God's Gift and can walk out and cure all ills. You can't. Healing is not about that. You are offering a complementary therapy, like many others, which will assist the healing process of your visitors. Never promise a cure, only assistance. Many patients come to Healers when all else has failed and, unfortunately, we are looked upon as a last resort; invariably it is far too late and all we can do is ease the situation.

Back to the theory. Where does it go and what does it do when it gets there? You will, hopefully, recall that when we were discussing the Auras we spoke of something that is closely allied to the Auras, but not really a part of them. The Etheric Body, which we described as being the Life Matrix; the scaffolding upon which the physical body is built. We reported that the 'life force' circulates through the Etheric, which then passes it on to each and every cell of our bodies; controlling the growth, and, logically speaking, the well being of each cell as well. You have passed the healing energy into the aura, which passes it to the Etheric, which, in turn, transmutes that energy into the 'life force' which reacts on the physical body, thereby occasioning the healing process. It is as simple as that.

Okay, you've got the hang of it, now what? No, you don't hang your shingle out and start saying you're a Healer. Turn your attention to family and friends; keep it within the family so to speak. It takes a great deal of Work, both by you and the Other Side, before you are in a position to offer your services. Those links have got to be really solid and well forged before you can deal with the public. This takes time and effort and cannot be done in just a few hours. It could take a very long time. As I said, look to those of the family and friends who won't deride what you are doing. Anything from bruises, headaches, aches, pains and even broken bones. However, if it is a broken leg let the local medical practitioner deal with it first and set it properly. The Healing that you provide will speed the healing process within the body and cause the bones to knit faster.

We have spoken quite a bit about Responsibility, one other aspect that has to be remembered is that of Respect. Respect for yourself, your patient, and the Other Side. You must, at all times, be comfortable. So should your patient. The fact that your patient complains of a bad toe or ankle does not mean that you have to get on your hands and knees and grovel around on the floor in order to get the Healing Energy to that part, demeaning yourself and the Other Side. Simply passing the energy into the Physical Aura and through to the Etheric will get the energy where it is needful in these cases. I well remember one of my patients coming to me limping and getting quite humorous because I had kept my hands around his ears whilst Working, but he was surprised when he had walked out normally.

The temperature differentials are not the only way to Work. As you become more and more in tune with the healers you might find yourself being inspired to place your hands in certain areas and also being impressed to put them elsewhere as time progresses. This is the way June Works. If you are none too sure with the hot and cold spots and are even unsure of the impressions you receive as to where to place your hands, as sometimes happens, a safe bet is always to place one hand on the area of the Physical Aura over the ganglion of nerves at the top of the spine, just below the neck. The other hand is placed over the area of the other major ganglion in the small of the back. The energy will permeate the entirety of the body from these two points.

Here in the U.K. Registered Spiritual Healers are permitted to go into Hospitals at the request of the patients. We have to check with whoever is in charge of the ward before going in; courtesy, if nothing else. No white coats, and we have to be in possession of our Healer Registration Cards. Then we simply sit beside the patient's bed and take hold of their hand and carry through the centring process and the healing power flows. No arm waving over the auras or such; just the simple hand touch. It Works just as well and does not draw any unnecessary attention from the other patients or members of staff.

Registration? Throughout the United Kingdom there are many Healing Associations; some described by their county or regional area. For instance, when I lived in Essex I was a member of the Essex Healers, and now I am a member of the Norfolk Healers Association. In order to qualify for full membership there is a form of apprenticeship which assess your suitability for such. The usual way is to make contact with the appropriate Association who will put you in contact with a Registered Healer in your immediate area, with whom you will be required to Work, under supervision, for at least one, if not two, years before being deemed qualified to Work alone. June, however, is qualified through her association with the Spiritualist's National Union and its Healing branch. There things are a little bit more involved inasmuch as she was required to sit examinations in the theory and practice of Healing as well as the two years probation.

Up to now we have dealt with the physical, but what about emotional trauma? This is where we turn our attention to the Mental/Emotional Aura. Your patient remarks about tension, stress or other such like problems, so you will be Working on this aura in regard to these types of complaints. However, there is no need to search for the temperature differentials, nor to aim at the two ganglions mentioned earlier. Simply set your hands anywhere on the surface of this aura and let the energy flow through you in exactly the same way as before.

There is one particular patient/client that we all tend to forget; ourselves. It is perfectly permissible to sit quietly and ask for healing for yourself. How can you be expected to do your job properly if you aren't fit to stand up, let alone Work on anybody else? Healer, heal thyself!

We have dealt with how the process Works and how you can use it, but being a Healer has a lot more to it than just being a 'psychic mechanic'. Remember Personal Responsibility, and Respect? Let us add a touch of Professionalism. This is not a game. You are dealing with other people's lives and whilst you are Working in any altered state of consciousness, those people who have come to you are in a vulnerable state; they are seeking your help. Anything that you say or do is going to have an impact on them in some way, shape or form. Consciously they may well ignore whatever is said, however, sub-consciously it will leave its mark.

I consider it very irresponsible forecast personal Death, Doom or Disaster to anyone. The reason being is that an unknown part of our brain tends towards the Self Fulfilment of Prophecy. I do not know how it works, except that I have seen it in action. As a simple example, someone was once told that they would have a red car. Much later, walking around the sales lots they were undecided between a number of cars until they eventually remembered the prophecy and decided that since they had been told they would have a red one, that was the one to buy. A silly example, I know, but it does illustrate the point. Tell someone that they will fall off their chair and they will; somehow.

At this point let me sound a cautionary note for those of you who are, like myself, of the masculine gender. A female patient. Never, ever give Healing to a woman on your own. Always have a third party present, preferably another woman. The shout of 'Rape!' is too easy to utter and extremely difficult to prove in denial. In regard to the lady's chest, stay away from it. Even if your hands are going over the Physical Aura as you seek out the temperature changed areas, the sight of your hands inches from her breasts can be very unsettling to some women. Forget that area totally. Should there be a need for Healing within the region of the heart and lungs, you can do it just as well from the back of the lady.

If you should find, at the end of a healing session, that you are feeling extremely tired, go back to the drawing board. Check out the forged links. You might find that they are not as secure as you perhaps thought. Your tiredness could well stem from the fact that you are giving of your own energy and not passing the energy from upstairs. In the U.K. we call this 'magnetic healing' and it is very common. One way to see this happening is through the sight of a patient leaving the session full of energy, but is completely depleted within two or three days. The patient is running on the healer's energy and will need to make frequent visits in order to be topped up; almost a vampire like need.

In regard to the Healing process, let us run through a typical Healing Session with a client who has made an appointment to come to you, and have a look at some suggestions in ensuring client comfort and relaxation. First of all have a look at the environment where you are going to be carrying out the Healing Session. Is it clean and tidy? At an average comfortable temperature? Assuming it is a sunny day, will the client be facing into the sun and therefore be disturbed by its brightness in their eyes? Remember, the sun moves across the sky and the brightness will move across the room. If it is cool outside is there somewhere to put their coat and bag? Somewhere where they can be sure that no-one will be digging in the pockets or rummaging through the contents; possibly on a chair in their line of sight. The client must feel safe and secure. A carafe of water to drink and some glasses. When you have finished you might feel a little dry, as might your client. Don't offer coffee or other hot drink since not only will you destroy the atmosphere clattering around with kettles and such, you may well have to end up with a super-market to cater to the many fads and fancies of people's tastes. Stick with plain water, and stay away from alcohol.

Then there is the problem of creating the right sort of atmosphere within the room. Music? Do you put on some sort of relaxing sounds? The problem is that what you may feel is the most wonderfully inspiring sound, someone else may find a discordant row. One person's rhapsody is another's cacophony. I would suggest that if you feel the need for the music, then, by all means, play it before your client arrives and then switch it off as they come to your door. Burning incense or fragrant oils? Many people have all sorts of allergies; some that they may not even be aware of. The nasal passages contain very sensitive organs and can pass substances quickly to the blood, which reacts on the physical. Plus there is the individual appreciation of what is a perfume and what is an horrendous stench? In simple terms, in order to make your client fully at ease, don't.

Which brings us to you. If you can fit it in, have a quick shower or a wash of the sweaty bits and go very, very easy on the deodorant if you feel the need to use it. Perfume or stench? Smokers, like me, should try not to have a 'fix' for about an hour before the client is due and a quick mouth rinse just before they arrive. In regard to your clothing, clean and tidy. No bows and frills that can come into contact with your client's body. Long hair? Get it up out of the way. You don't want the hair dragging across the client's face if you have to lean forward. No rattling chains or pendants that will disturb your patient's relaxation by clanking in their ear. Soft soled comfortable shoes? You may well be standing for some time and moving around your client. The clump of foot falls and creaking leather can be very off-putting. The client's chair should be placed on some sort of carpeting in such a way that you can move all around it without any mountaineering requirements. Other free standing chairs are in reasonably close proximity so that, should you find you are going to be in one particular area for some time, you can, very quietly, bring one forward so that you can sit comfortably and not get backache. Have a footstool or cushions handy, just in case your client has short legs.

You and your environment are now ready for the client. When they arrive welcome them politely and courteously and usher them into the room. Help them off with their coats and take their bags, placing them fully in the view of the client. The only other thing you might invite the client to remove is their shoes if they so wish. Nothing else. The aim is for client comfort. Sit them in the chair and then sit opposite them, say six to eight feet away. Neither tables nor desks to act as a barrier between you. In your best compassionate manner ask them what they believe their problem to be. Have they seen their Doctor? What was the diagnosis? Make a mental note of what is reported; remember it, don't write it down (yet). Go into an explanation that the Healing you are offering is designed to assist the work of the Medical Profession and should certainly not be regarded as a form of replacement therapy. Be politely insistent that if the patient is undergoing some form of medication as prescribed by the Doctor etc. then they must continue with it. The Healing must be recognised as a complementary therapy the same as any other, and not as an alternative to medicine.

From this point, June and I advise the client of what will be going on physically. The client is invited to get themselves comfortable, bringing in the footstool or cushions as required. Once they are settled you advise that you are going to stand behind them for a few moments and then move forward and, very gently, place your fingertips on their shoulders; thereby letting the client know that you are ready to start. Lifting the hands off you will then be Working on the appropriate aura and will not touch their person again until the very end, when you will then stand behind the client again and, even more gently, place the finger tips lightly back on their shoulders to let them know that the process has come to an end. You will then step back and await the client's responsive movement.

Also advise the client that they may, or may not, feel anything whilst you are Working. If they should feel tingles, heat, coldness, pressure changes, they should recognise that these feelings are natural effects of the energy flow and there is no need for alarm. Even if they feel nothing at all, that doesn't mean that nothing is happening; its just happening very subtly. If they do find themselves dozing off, tell them to go with it. Sleep is a wonderful healer in it's own right. Assure them that you will not allow them to fall off the chair.

You are now ready to start. Stand back behind the client, centre yourself as has already been described, have whatever silent words you feel are appropriate to you. When you feel things beginning to happen, step forward and lightly place your fingers on the client's shoulders. On to the appropriate aura and things will run of their own accord. You might find, whilst you are in neutral and the Healing is running, you will receive some diagnostic information. File it in your memory and keep your mouth shut.

Process over, stand behind the client, fingers tip very, very gently on the shoulders to show them that you've finished. Step back and have your 'thank you' words with upstairs, which will 'release' them and you. Move around to the front and keep a close eye on your client until they start to move of their own volition. Offer them a drink of water and take one yourself. This simple action helps you both to 'earth' yourselves back in this world. Check on the client's response and how they are feeling. If you have received any diagnostic information, check in your mental file as to whether they told you of it before you started. If you blurt out that it is a nasty cancer on their left lung, or in the right breast, or the heart valve is out of phase, you could well end up needing to resort to Medical First Aid as your client has a quick heart attack with the shock. It doesn't help.

If you have received some other type of information aimed at the client, get back to the drawing board. If you look again at Diagram 3 in Chapter 5 you will see that the Healers are at Point 6 and that the Guides are at Point 7. The two links are totally separate. If you are Working the Healing link, there is no way that you can also be Working the Guidance link. Something is not quite right with the links and they may well have to be reforged. Besides which, some people may well use the Healing as an excuse for getting 'Messages'. Horses for courses; don't mix healing and clairvoyance.

Advise you client that there is the possibility that for the next day or two it might appear that the Healing has aggravated the problem as it 'plays up'. This is perfectly normal and is a sure indication that 'something' has happened. I have often heard it referred to as a part of the 'Healing Curve'. It will ease off and they will feel an improvement after a while. Gently assist your client back into their coats and pass them their other bits and pieces and ease them out of the door.

Before you do anything else, get some notes down and keep a written record, not on a disc or computer, of who the client was, the complaint that brought them to you, any diagnosis you picked up, plus any comments that you feel it may be necessary to help you should they call again. Partner's name, children, job, etc.. You can check these before your client returns next time.

At the turn of the Century, Healers used to spend a lot of time and energy wiping their hands over the patient's aura to cleanse it of the disease and flicking the 'whatever' across the room. It all looks very theatrical, but actually does nothing, except, make the Healer look a bit of an idiot. Remember our comments about cleansing auras? That sort of process is no longer needed.

Similarly, Healers were required to wash their hands in a bowl of water between each patient. Since the healing takes place on the appropriate aura, how have the hands got dirty? I have even been present where the Healer's hands have been passed through a burning candle flame to cleanse them. It does nothing for the Healing Process, but, obviously, looks 'good' from the egotistical point of view. Pain? Not me! Remember? Devout coward.

There is another aspect that may well bring itself to your notice as you progress. The use of colour in your Work. When you are stood passing the healing through to your client you may well be inspired to visualise a colour being directed to the effected areas or an overall colour over the whole of the person.

As a general outline I list some of the colours that we have used and the reasons. Remember, the list is not exhaustive and you are best to be advised by those who are Working through you

Indigo Blue	Calms Inflammation
Blue	General Cooling
Pale Green	Emotional Tranquilliser
Green	Neutral Building
Grey	Calming, Creating Balance
Yellow	Mentally Stimulating
Scarlet/Orange	Stimulating (only below waist)
Violet/Purple	Subduing
Light Blue	Spiritual Healing
Pink	Love, Compassion

You will have noticed that we stipulated that Scarlet/Orange should only be used below the waist. These shades carry an extra energy phase and we do not want to put any energy strain on the heart; so, be warned. Personal Responsibility again.

Note: the colours have a different meaning than when we were looking at the auras.

72

On average an individual Healing session will last about forty to forty-five minutes from the client coming in to their leaving. Give yourself a little time before you see your next client, say fifteen minutes between each.

We come to the vexed question of payment. The actual cost of Healing is, simply, nothing. However, you have given of your time and skills and you might consider that requires a fee. Your choice, of course. There is a metaphysical aspect, however, to what you have been doing. Energy has passed to the client and requires a reciprocation. Giving demands a receiving in order to harmonise the process. Neither June nor I will make any charge for Healing, however, when asked, we will advise that there is a suitable plate near the door for people to make any donation that may wish; offering the client the right of free choice.

You're now in a Working mode as a Healer. I would suggest that you don't go around telling everyone that you are a Healer and looking for business. By all means, let it be known that you are one, but do not offer to Work on anyone. Let those that need it come to you. Let them make the first move; psychologically it is far more effective and allows the energy to run smoother.

There is more than one way that you can use you abilities in Healing. You don't even have to see your patient, let alone know them. In the U.K. we call it 'Absent Healing', others refer to it as 'Distant Healing'.

In many Spiritualists' Churches they have what is known as a Healing Book. People can write down a name and a brief description of the malady and at some point in each service there is a Healing Minute where prayers are said on behalf of all those listed in the pages. Their names are not read out because it is not necessary. Apart from any Spiritual link that may be a part of the religious aspect, there is also a psychic link with the named patient through the action of the writer who, obviously, has some form of connection with the patient. As an individual Healer you can operate along similar lines and keep some form of book with the names of people who need help in it. Enter any names that you feel are necessary. Obviously you can enter the briefest of

73

details of your clients. We sometimes get telephone calls from people asking for us to send Healing to this or that person that the caller knows; the call is the link with the patient, even if it wasn't them calling.

At the end of you Healing Day, sit quietly for a few moments, holding your book or list of names of people who need help and mentally send a few words upstairs to your healing guides for healing for them all in accordance with their individual needs. Say thank you and put the book away until the next time.

When do you actually know that you are a fully fledged Healer? It is very difficult to determine. Watch how many people begin to come to you for Healing. Are they sporadic, a steady trickle, or lining up at the door? Whichever it is doesn't prove anything. There are some fantastic Healers who may only see half a dozen people once or twice in a year. There are also some very mediocre Healers who have a constant stream of people standing on their doorstep.

Remember, in order to become a Registered Healer we have to be a Probationary Healer, Working regularly under the guidance of a fully Registered Healer, for at least two consecutive years and can only be assessed as competent by that same Healer and passed for acceptance by the Committee of that particular Healing Association.

Within the Spiritualists' National Union, in addition to the two years, there is the requirement to sit, and pass, a number of examinations on the theory and practice of Healing, plus an examination on anatomy. It could help to know where the spleen and livers are and have some idea of their functions.

However, in short, don't be too much concerned as to egotistical demands to have a label or two. Those who can, do.

Chapter 8

The Tarot

Many people who come to you are seeking healing; not just of the physical body, but of the mind as well. The vast majority of our problems stem from our sense of the fear of the unknown. Our imaginings cause all sorts of problems for us. Anything which can bring some form of hope and possible understanding to our situation can only be beneficial. I have found that the Tarot, read intelligently and with compassion for the sitter, is just such an instrument and make no apologies for placing it beside the usual concepts of healing.

All the Tarot books that I have ever seen go to great lengths in the first pages to establish the antiquity of the origins of Tarot. Some say that it originated in Afghanistan, some say the Middle East, others pin-point it to ancient Egypt. Personally, I don't give a hoot where it came from. It is sufficient for me that it is here and that it Works as far as I am concerned. The last time I counted, some years ago, there were over 350 different designs of pack, most of them very recent The list has probably grown a lot longer by now. Each different design fulfils a need for somebody.

However, not all packs of cards are Tarot. For instance, Jamie Sam's and David Carson's excellent *Medicine Cards* are a wonderful tool to gain insights about yourself and your immediate environment, as are *The Sacred Path* cards, also by Jamie Sams. But they are not Tarot Cards. Do not, however, let this blind you to the benefits of Working with them. On occasion I will freely use either, or both, of these pack as an adjunct to a Tarot Reading where the occasion warrants it. For instance, if a particular reading shows the need to investigate a specific matter in greater detail than the spread is showing I will take the other deck of cards and use that instead of closing the spread I have partially laid out and get down to the real nuts and bolts of the situation. Not always pleasant for the person receiving the reading.

In general terms, I believe that we need to be very aware that no person can tell another what to do. We are looking at Personal Responsibility. When a Tarot Reader (or Tarotist, as I prefer to call them) sits to give somebody a reading, that other person's life is, potentially, in the Tarotist's hands. The person receiving the reading will be very vulnerable to whatever suggestions are made. Most people come for readings when they are in a stressed condition and are seeking a light at the end of whatever tunnel they are currently in. Many come when they are in such financial difficulties that they don't know which way to turn, and can ill afford the financial exchange of energy. Therefore there is the Tarotist's need to recognise their own Personal Responsibility.

When I initially gave a reading, here in our home in England, there was no charge, as such, for the service. However, I do expect the sitter to make good the expenses incurred by me. All of my readings are taped, because they contain a depth of detail over the period of the next few months and there is no way that the sitter could be expected to remember all that I have said. I did expect the sitter to pay for the C90 tape. Currently £1, or $1.50. If they then wished to make a donation of however much that was down to them. If they could afford another £1 or more, well and good. If not, so be it. As an anomaly to this I am reminded of a Tarotist of my acquaintance who advertised her abilities at £25 (approximately $37.50) and had a steady few requests. When she put the price up to £35 (approximately $52.50) she was overwhelmed with the response. Same reader, same reading, same cards, different price. There is nothing as strange as people.

I have made a passing comment on 'the exchange of energy'; money. A Tarotist giving a reading is using their abilities and energy for the benefit of the other person. The other person is receiving that energy and should, therefore, give of themselves in return. All things require a balanced interflow between the parties involved. In our current society money is used as a tool to facilitate such an exchange. Look at many bank notes and you

76

will see the words, "I promise to pay the bearer, on demand, the sum of...". Money is just a promise, an obligation, from the issuer. The note, itself, has no value. It is the idea behind it that gives it a value.

However, I now hire a room in two centres, reasonably local to my home, but still either 10 or 20 miles away. Rent has to be paid for each of them when I use them, plus I have to maintain the car, put petrol in the tank, carry a tape recorder, keep a stock of tapes, and use a microphone which uses batteries. Occasionally I will even drive to someone's home to give a reading. This all has to be covered in the cost of the reading. Balance the books!

Back to the Tarot. I use the Rider Waite design because I can relate to it and it 'speaks' to me. Another pack will speak to somebody else and be equally effective for them. I am of the opinion that no one should buy a pack for somebody else to use. One of the myths in my youth was that you couldn't buy your own pack; it had to be a gift from someone. I would suggest that the would be reader should go to a well stocked shop and browse through all the designs they have available and see if any particular design leaps out at them. A number of shops that I know keep a photograph album style folder with four or five cards from each pack on display for this very reason. The pack that does catch your eye could well be the one for you. I also find that the Rider Waite pack can be very gentle and compassionate towards the person receiving the reading, whereas some other packs I have used tend to be a trifle brutal and unfeeling for the person in their dilemma.

My very first pack was a Marseilles. Most of the cards were swirls of the hint of the suit and required an extensive memory to remember what each design could mean. It hurt my brain. They didn't last long. The Rider Waite, on the other hand, has a picture on every card which could relate to the idea of the meaning of the card. A glance at the picture and you are on your way.

Let's get down to the basics of Tarot. The true Tarot deck comprises of 78 cards, which are unequally divided into 5 suits. 4 of these suits each contain 14 cards and are related to the

77

ordinary 4 suits of 13 cards in a 52 card pack of playing cards. Whereas the ordinary suits are of hearts, clubs, diamonds and spades, the Tarot uses Cups, Wands, Pentacles (Coins) and Swords respectively. The ordinary pack goes from the Ace to the King. A Rider-Waite Tarot suit, however, goes from the Ace to the Ten, then through a Page, a Knight, a Queen, and then a King. These are all known as the Minor Arcana.

The fifth suit is known as the Major Arcana and comprises of 22 individual cards which are related, one to the other. It is this fifth suit with which we will be mainly dealing in these pages. It is said that the 78 Cards of the Tarot are the story of an average life span of a person. The 56 Cards of the Minor Arcana are the padding, or descriptive narratives, unessential to the main story which is contained in the 22 Cards of the Major Arcana. The Major Arcana is often referred to as The Journey of the Fool. A person passing from birth to death. We will use my version of this story as a very brief introduction to the cards of the Major Arcana.

The essential Spirit unknowingly makes the descent from the Spirit Realms, and therefore may be characterised as the Fool (Card Numbered 0). It quickly needs to adjust to the physical environment. Coming to terms with the four elements of Earth, Fire, Air and Water, which are portrayed upon the table of the Magician (Card 1).The instinctive, almost intuitive, desire for life comes from within, The High Priestess (Numbered 2). The new life draws its initial sustenance, both mental and physical, from the Mother, portrayed as the Empress (3). The second contact comes with the Father, who instils discipline and rules, the Emperor (4). The time comes for an expansion of knowledge and the child is released into the world in order to attend school and learn all that it needs for its future from the Teachers. The Hierophant (5). Schooling comes to an end and choices have to be made, not only in regard to an occupation, but in regard to a mate as well, shown in the questions of the Lovers (6).

The person moves out of the familiar environment of the home by way of the Chariot (7). Strength (8) comes from the establishment of a partner and new home. As the new couple set to developing their personal relationship there is a tendency for them to become insular and withdrawn from the rest of the world, alone on their personal mountain, they are the Hermit (9). The time comes when they are no longer self sufficient, and need the company and stimulus of other people and changes come under the impetus of the Wheel of Fortune (10). Justice (11), rears its head as they come to understand what is right and wrong for the two of them. Compromise comes in the form of the self-sacrifice inherent in the Hanged Man (12). Maturity comes with the responsibility of caring for a family and the changes that result in the Death (13) of the previous life. Adjustments to the new situation bring harmony through Temperance (14). Life settles into a rut and habits take a serious hold under the influence of the Devil (15).

Realisation comes of the need to break free like a bolt out of the blue, shown in the Tower (16). The dream demands to become a reality and the impetus of the Star (17) drives the urge for the future to be built. Setting forth on the yellow brick road, the individual, or couple, stride for the horizon, through the Twin Pillars of Wisdom in the Moon (18). It is their decision, the Sun (19), whether they make the Dancing of the Dreamtime Awake a fact or not. The life draws to a close and they spend time in nostalgic review of the past. Have they lived it to the full or frittered it away? Only they can decide under their perception of self Judgement (20). Physical death claims the Spirit and it returns to the Spirit Realms, older and wiser, having evolved a stride further it moves into a whole new ball game; the World (21). In the fullness of time the Spirit may decide to make the Journey of the Fool again.

You now have to make an important decision in regard to understanding the meanings of each Tarot card. When you buy a pack, in the box is a booklet of some description. They all seem to follow the same sort of pattern. A brief outline of the antiquity of the cards; a list of the meanings of each card; and one or more specimen layouts. I would suggest that you enjoy the first part, if that is your thing. Study the last until you are sure of the layout you find comfortable. Then throw the booklet away. The reason for this is that the list of meanings relates to the mind of the person who either composed the cards or wrote the booklet. You are not them, therefore the cards may mean something different to you, even if it is somewhat similar. Tarot is a personal tool for each individual. The hardest person to give a reading to is another Tarotist. You will be reading the cards your way and the other will be reading the cards their way as they watch what you are doing. Few Tarotists can keep their mouth shut in a reading situation, even if they are not doing the reading.

Which brings us to the next point in doing readings. The gift of the gab. Patter. A good Tarotist has to have the ability to keep talking and linking back and forth across the spread making it an understandable story and keeping things interesting for the sitter. You also have to be prepared for questions, often at the most awkward of times in the midst of a spread.

It is no good firing barrages of accurate information at your sitter if they have gone to sleep or are totally bemused by what you are saying. Be prepared to throw in the odd wise-crack or joke to stimulate the sitter; however, use discretion. If the cards are indicating serious financial, emotional, matrimonial, or legal problems; don't. In these instances, always remember compassion and try to put yourself in the place of the sitter and how you would feel in their position at the news of such a possibility. Remember, that last word. Possibility. Nothing is cut and dried in Life; except death and taxes. No matter what reading you are doing, you are only looking at the way things stand at the time of the reading. If, having finished your reading, the sitter walks out in a fit of pique and throws themselves in front of a bus (which wasn't in the reading) then the whole scenario has changed. The time line has been broken and little of what you may have said originally will have any relevance.

If the sitter leaves and continues along the path indicated, then the influences of the cards turned will run their course. But if the sitter makes a major adjustment in the use of their freewill then the time line will change and your reading will be as nothing, unless you were shown that the possibility of the change would occur, which, in these circumstances, are unlikely.

Another point to watch is not to do a reading for someone too often. Tarot, like any other activity, can become addictive. A young lady of my acquaintance would sit up in bed each morning, turn a card to see what the day would bring then, if she didn't like what it inferred, would turn over and not get up for the rest of the day. Remember, many that come for a reading are in a vulnerable and stressed condition. Whilst being compassionate, you also have to be strong. If you are charging a dollar a minute for your time, as we experienced on a visit to the USA, you are going to make a lot of money out of that person. A true Tarotist will only see any person a maximum of once every three months.

In my opinion, to give a reading for a period in excess of three months is pushing the realms of possibility a bit far. There are so many influences on our lives that we can act, or react, to; any one of which can alter the current time line.

Whilst the Tarotist does hold a very responsible position in giving the reading, we must always remember that the Tarot and the Tarotist is neither a God nor Goddess.

Let us assume that you have been to the shop and selected your pack of cards. You have a nice, pretty box, probably wrapped in cellophane and you get home, have done your chores and are now ready to make inroads on the deck. You are sat comfortably in a chair with a table of some description in front of you; perhaps a coffee or tea perched safely beside you. Now what? The first problem, quite often, is getting into the box. You scrabble around at the edges of the shrink-wrap, split a nail or two, curse vehemently, then have to get up and find a knife or a pair of scissors to break in on the cards. Then the removed packaging has to be dealt with. Bits of it get everywhere and you end up getting the Hoover, or something similar, to collect up all the shards and put it in the garbage.

Tarot is no less a part of 'Magic' than anything else. In all magic there is an element of chaos; better the chaos before you Work than during it. Okay, you're now settled, again. You start to read. Rules are introduced. The pack must be kept in a silk cloth. You must sleep with it under your pillow each night. You must only shuffle the cards yourself. Never let anyone else touch them unless they are simply cutting the cards with their left hand on your table. If these ideas appeal to you, have fun. They certainly add a sense of mystique to what you are doing. For me, its all bovine manure.

My cards are kept in an old Kodak Brownie 127 camera case with a snap fastener, together with a miniature microphone, extension lead and a spare battery or two. It all fits in very nicely, thank you. As for working on a silken cloth? My basic spread contains anywhere between 37 and 55 cards. That's a big piece of silk. Quite often, whilst my sitter relaxed in a nice easy chair beside me, I would sit cross-legged on the floor and spread them out across the carpet in front of me. Try not to have your sitter across the other side of the table, or whatever, from you. It puts a barrier between you. A management/peasant confrontation. Having them beside you indicates that you are 'on their side' and makes things easier for the sitter.

Talking about the sitters ease, remember they have come to you for help. Be aware of the atmosphere you are creating in your room, wherever. Have you lit some incense? Do you think it is wonderful and soothing? Does your sitter agree? What if they have an allergy to whatever your are wafting around the room? Music? Gentle and soft in the background with the aim of soothing? One persons symphony is another person's cacophony. Are the windows lined with crystals to cascade rainbows around the room? As the sun moves around so the rainbows will move about the room and shine in your, and the sitter's, eyes causing irritation. Think things through.

Back to the Tarot. Firstly, you've got to establish some sort of rapport with your cards. You got to really know those cards. How do we do this? Look at them. Both in their suits and individually. Don't, whatever you do, get impatient. This is going to take time. The more time you spend with the cards, singularly or together, the better you will come to understanding them.

In running through the cards as we progress through these pages I must emphasise that these are my understandings of the cards and may not, in the longer term, be yours or anybody else's, but we do need some common ground from which to work through our subject, bearing in mind, also, that I am basing this on the Rider Waite design.

In the Minor Arcana, the suit of Cups tends to deal with the emotions, Wands relate to energy, Pentacles to the physical, and Swords to the mind. As a further spur, look at them in relation to the Elements. Cups hold water; Pentacles are physical objects, therefore are of the earth; you feed a fire with wood, hence Wands are part of fire. A Sword slices through the air.

Take one of the suits and spend some time getting the overall feel of that particular suit. You should be able to see, fairly quickly, how I have arrived at the relationships I have just mentioned. But, don't just take my word for it. They may not be right for you in the longer term. Don't skimp the intricate detail in the card. Its there for a reason. Get your glasses on. Get out a magnifier. Have a proper look. In the V of Swords, for instance, describe the clouds. What of the two people who are standing with their back to you? The look on the face of the third person? The mountains on the horizon? Why five swords and only three people? In the Ace of Wands, why is it sprouting? Green flames about it? A white castle? Guarding what and why? The trees and river? Look at the minutiae, the tiny detail, of each card. See if you can see some sort of storyline in each card, then lay out the whole suit and look for an overall storyline in that suit. Let your imagination run riot and have some fun with your mental gymnastics. Enjoy the whole learning experience.

June has recently spent some time with the Tarot; without any pretence of becoming a Tarotist - her mediumship keeps breaking through and she's off and running with stuff that the cards do not and cannot tell and invariably has little or nothing to do with the actual reason for the reading. However, she decided to sleep with them under her pillow. Vivid and incomprehensible dreams seemed to be the result. I've never done it so cannot give an answer to the effectiveness, or otherwise, of this method of establishing a rapport. Give it a whirl, if you wish, and see what happens. You've nothing to lose and, possibly, a lot to gain. Who knows? Try it with the whole pack, one suit, or just one card. See what happens. Enjoy however you learn.

Once you feel secure with the Minor Arcana you can move into the Big Kids Game. The Major Arcana. The learning process is exactly the same. Look at the card and all the detail. Why has V the Hierophant got two people kneeling in front of him? Why is he holding his hand in such a way? What of the trees behind III the Empress? And the wheat about her? Question, question, question. As you do, so answers will begin to appear. Where from? Your subconscious? The Racial Group Soul? Somewhere else? Aliester Crowley used the concept of a Spirit, or Guardian, of Tarot, whom he named as Hru, Lord of Tarot. Does it really matter? As long as the answers prove true to yourself, go with it.

Which brings me to the point about the most difficult person for whom you will be asked to do a reading. Yourself. We have a serious problem inasmuch as when we sit to do a reading for ourselves we are up to our necks in our personal desires for the right answers to fit in with our personal hopes, dreams, fears, and wishes. The mind will, invariably, get in the way and colour whatever we see in the cards. The cards, themselves, will show Truth, but we get in the way and, often, mis-interpret what we see.

If you do give yourself a reading make a note not only of what you see, but also what the actual card was that you read. You will then be able to look back and see if you read the cards truly at the time or if you got in the way. It can be a valuable lesson.

Okay, you are now comfortable with the cards having established a rapport with them and its time to leap in the deep end. Laying out a spread. The most common spread seems to be the Celtic Cross, which is favoured by all the books and booklets I have come across. The way I Work, I let the sitter shuffle the cards until they are comfortable with how it feels in their hands and I then offer them the opportunity to cut the cards as many times as they like (with either hand, it doesn't bother me or my Tarot), then return the complete deck to me and I peel the cards off, one at a time, and lay them out. But, you do whatever you feel most comfortable with, just so long as you end up with the layout in front of you.

Let's have a look at the overall layout first and then talk it through. See Diagram 4. Card Position 1, is termed the Significator and details what is significant in the sitter's life at this point in time.

Card 2, is what crosses the sitter, showing either conflict or support for the current situation.

Position 3 crowns the sitter. The ultimate goal or destiny, or their ideal aim.

4 is beneath the sitter. The foundation of the past which has produced the identity and personality of the sitter.

5 represents the recent past and the effect it has had upon the current situation.

6 is the future influences that are likely in the near future.

7 shows the present position of the sitter within the situation.

8 shows other factors that may have an effect on the situation.

9 shows the inner feelings, emotions and intuition of the sitter.

10 reveals the end result of everything represented by the preceding cards.

It is a good spread and will cover most situations that the Tarotist will come across.

However, as I Worked with it I kept getting the feeling that it was unstable. This was easily remedied when I took the last four cards and spread them horizontally across the bottom as a base upon which to stand the Cross. See Diagram 5.

Things went along quite nicely for a time until the niggle set in that there was a problem with the time factor. Its all very well saying that something will happen in the fullness of time. But what is the fullness of time? Okay, time is a man-made concept,

DIAGRAM 4

THE CELTIC CROSS

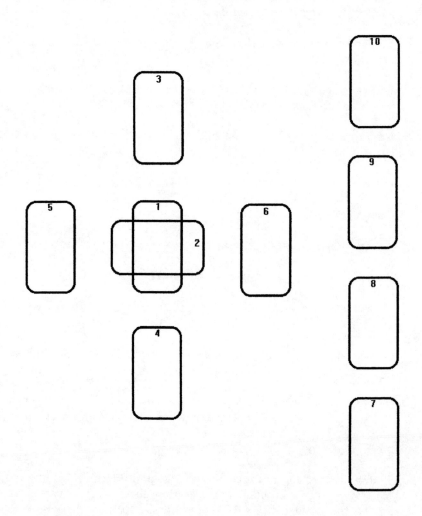

Diagram 5

AN AMENDED CELTIC CROSS

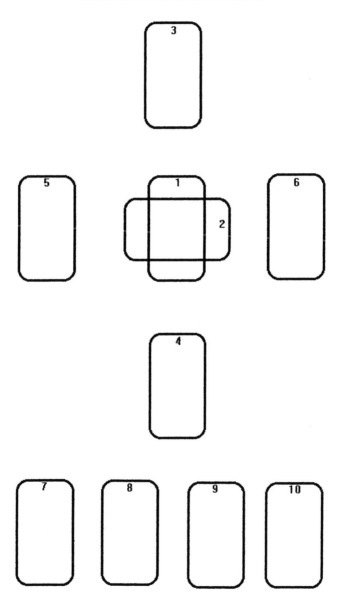

Diagram 6

A ONE MONTH CROSS

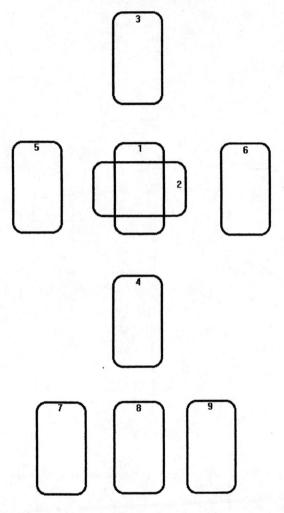

(The Amended Celtic Cross Card 10 becoming Card 1 of the Next Months' Cross)

which those in the Spirit, or other, realms do not comprehend. But we are here, now, living in a world governed by time. 'Soon' for those others may be a decade for us. There had to be a way.

With a few protestations, The Merlin showed me a way. Lay out the first 9 cards as shown in Diagram 6, slipping the bottom three slightly to the right to keep the balance and stipulate that these cards represent the month that has just ended, or is about to end. Take the 10th card and lay it as card number 1 in another Celtic Cross to the right of the first. This Cross represents the next month. Similarly, take the 10th card of this Cross and lay it as card number 1 for a further Celtic Cross to the right of the second Cross, for the following month. A further Cross may be laid to the right of this last, giving you a total four month spread. A final card is then drawn and placed, on its own, either above or below the whole spread, depending on how much room you have available to lay the card. This is the overall card representing the entirety of the spread.

Problem? Of course. You have laid out 37 cards, nearly half the pack. Its a bit limiting to expect a true answer from such confines. Even if you do decide to dualise each card by having reversed cards meaning something different to the normal upright - I don't, but to each his own. How do we get around this? Simple. Use two packs. Shuffle them together. You now have 156 cards to work with. 37 from 156 is less than a quarter of the packs.

Personal Responsibility. No man can tell another what to do. The Merlin suggested that I treat the cards along the lines of Astrology. Look at the influences portrayed by the cards, not what the person is actually doing. He pointed out that I have enough problems trying to live my own life, without trying to live other people's lives. That is their problem. However, a knowledge of the influences around, and within, a person at any given time allows for a more harmonious reaction to be reached in any decision making process. For example, if we know that during a particular period of time there is liable to be a lot of aggression and misunderstandings about, we can, if we wish defer any major decision making process until that has passed.

The other point I also stipulate to my sitters is that I don't want to know what they are seeking in the cards. I don't want to know what their problems are. Come in, sit down and get comfortable, do you need a drink of water? Shuffle the cards and on we go. The reason for this is the very human one of wanting to help the sitter, therefore it is a part of our nature that we want things to be okay for the sitter. We might, just might, tend to become over-involved and consequently colour our reading for our 'friend', the sitter. If you don't know, you cant tell. You can only give an unbiased reading, which will be far more effective for the sitter. As the Theosophists state, 'There is nothing higher than Truth'.

Back to the actual spread. The standard definitions of the placements still felt a bit loose for my liking. The Merlin and I spent some time checking, and double checking, developing some new definitions and the results have proved to be very comfortable and practical in the time since.

Firstly, let us set some parameters for the spread. To start we have to look at the date of when we doing the reading. If it is within the first two weeks of a month, the first Cross will be the preceding month. If you have passed the middle of the current month, then the first Cross will be the month that you are in. Before we can 'shoot' into the future, we need to anchor things in the past. Read what has already happened in the life of the sitter. Get them to acknowledge the rightness of it and you are ready to jump into the unknown.

On occasion, however, you might find that it is totally opposite to what you have read. Accept it. There are times in a person's life when they have to make their decisions on blind faith alone. This may well be one of them. The Tarot is not 'speaking', therefore abandon the whole reading and ease you sitter, gently, out; perhaps to return in a few weeks time, when the Tarot may be able to help. On these rare occasions I make no formal charge for anything. They do not get the tape, and it can be wiped and reused. Be honest with your sitter and you'll probably gain a friend.

If you have used the first Cross as the preceding month, the second Cross will be the current month. If the first was the current month, then the second Cross will be the following month. And so on through the spread. Treat each Cross as a separate entity in your mind, but be prepared to leap backwards and forwards across the whole spread, linking items and situations wherever possible. Remember to keep it interesting and lively for your sitter. I find it easier to turn and speak of each card separately, rather than laying all 37, or more, cards and then start reading. The sitter is then able to keep pace with where you are in the spread.

This is where you might need the other cards I spoke of earlier. You are talking of the influences halfway through the 37 cards, when your sitter throws a question at you. You are faced with a number of possibilities. Stop the reading, gather the cards up again and start all over from that point; ask the sitter to remember and raise the question later; draw one of the other packs of cards (even another pack of Tarot) and take that as a tangent line of questioning. I find it is better to ask the sitter to remember and deal with it later. But, each to their own.

The placement definitions in Diagram 6. Cards numbered 1 and 2 are the major influences for the month.

Card 3 can be either the Mental influence, or the Spiritual influence, throughout the month. As you meet and greet your sitter you will soon learn to read their body language, etc., and intuit whether they are materialistic or spiritually inclined. On occasions, however, the first card to be placed here will give you a nudge to which it is.

Number 4 can be either the Emotional influences, or the Physical influence. The decision on Card 3, will lead you to the correct usage in this position.

5 shows the influences over the first half of the month.

6 shows the influences over the second half of the month.

7 describes the sitter's Inner influences; subconscious; spirit within, etc..

8 shows the influence of the Environment upon the sitter's situation. Relatives; friends; fellow workers; etc..

9 determines the sitter's Hopes or Fears in that month's situation.

Remember, Card 10 becomes Card 1, to join with 2, in the next month's spread.

As I said, the final card of the whole spread shows the general influence of the whole period. Having gone through the major phase of my type of reading, I move on to the supplementary spreads. The Four Month spread may well have answered your sitter's question, but, there again, it may not. This second phase is about dealing with specific questions. Shuffle the cards and fan them, face down, across the floor or table. Ask the sitter to think of their questions. Take one of them, and hold it silently, firmly in their mind. Whilst they are holding the thought invite them to draw, at random, any three cards and pass them to you.

The first card represents the influences that were present in regard to their question in the Past. The second, represents the Current influences in regard to their question. The third, and final, card represents the Future influences and possible outcome of their question, as things stand at that time. An idea of the Time frame can be surmised by looking at how far back the sitter needs to go to get to the influences shown in the Past card, then take the same amount of time into the Future. That is, approximately, how far forward before that influence is in vogue. It is not your responsibility to know what the question was, and you should tell the sitter that. However, for their own sake, suggest that they give themselves a word or two to act as a clue to exactly what the question was that they were asking when they come to play the tape back later. Gather in the three cards that they drew, lose them in the fanned pack, gather the pack together and then re-fan them in readiness for the next question.

I tend to keep going for as long as it takes them to ask all their questions. You could even suggest, in order to help the sitter, that there are three types of question. Those they ask at the time of the reading; then there are those they think of when they are halfway home; and, finally, there are those that they remember just as they are dropping off to sleep that night. Let them, therefore, try and dredge up the last two types of question and bring them forward to the 'now'. Also stipulate that the questions must be about the sitter, and or their spouse or 'marriage partner', since, hopefully, the two are one and what effects one will effect the other. Forget the kids, and granny. It is their reading, nobody else's. A question about someone else may produce an answer which the sitter might construe as horrific, but to the actual person concerned, it may be wonderful and the best thing ever.

When the sitter is 'questioned out' move into the final phase. In the broadest, most general outline, have a look at the next twelve months; starting from the month of the reading. This is done by getting them to shuffle again, just as they did when we first started the reading. Cutting if they wish, until they are satisfied with the cards, and then returning them to you. Peel off the cards into the normal Cross of 9 cards. The definitions and placements remain the same, except that the card to the left of the Cross represents the first six months, and the one to the right shows the second six months. (Cards 5 and 6 in Diagram 6). In both the first and third phases of a reading, I might suggest that you don't leave your sitter with the forecast of 'doom' hanging over them. There are enough cards still in the pack to shoot forward another month or two (or a year or two) for you to continue and find the silver lining behind the dark cloud in front of them. You have come to the end of the reading and you now have to ease the sitter, gently, out. Irrespective of the forthcoming influences don't ask your sitter if they are 'happy' with their reading. I suggest you ask if they are 'satisfied' with what you've reported. Having just advised your sitter that there is the strong possibility of family feuds, for instance, which will bring a lot of aggravation into their lives; they would hardly be 'happy' with the news.

Diagram 7

OPTION SPREAD

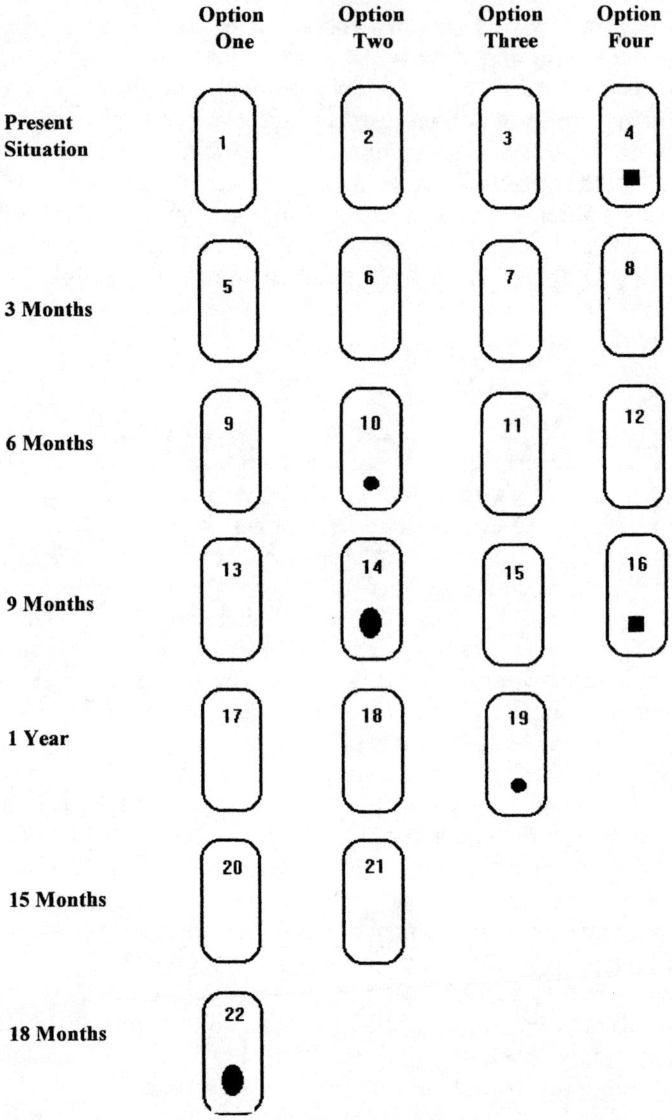

A final hint or two. If your sitter then talks to you about a return visit, aim for somewhere within the last month of your first spread so that as one runs out the other takes over. As I've said, try not to aim too far into the future with the first spread. There are too many possible variables to contend with. Remember what I said about them throwing themselves under a bus? It can all change due to some wilful action, or even a spur of the moment fit of pique, on the part of the sitter.

Always turn whatever card is next in such a way that you see it before the sitter does. For instance, the Death card can produce some problems when you come to turn it. The word alone can send your sitter into a panic. When it does turn up have a few explanatory words to tell of its significance. Hold the card in your hand, with one finger along the bottom of the card hiding the actual word Death, and ask the sitter to look closely at the card. The picture shows a young child, an adolescent, a mature person and an elderly person. Explain that the young child dies to become the adolescent, the adolescent dies to become the mature person, and so on. Therefore it is the death of one to become the other. It doesn't therefore mean that the sitter is going to physically die. The sitter is facing an end and a beginning to a situation in their lives. Invite them, compassionately, to revel in it; they are growing. You can then lay the card in its appropriate place in the spread and move on to the next and finish the readings.

There is one other spread that I rarely use because of the seriousness of the implications that run with it. I call it the Options Spread and for which you must be using Two Packs together. I say 'rarely' because it has tremendous ramifications if misunderstood. Based on the concept that no one can tell another what to do, how can you advise someone to follow a particular path when there are so many in front of them? What happened to free-will?

Assume for the moment that someone has come to see you because they see that they are standing at a major cross-roads in their life and are uncertain as to which way to turn. I preclude such basic things as selling their house and buying somewhere else, or leaving their partner and running off with another person. That is not what this spread is about. This is really serious stuff. Let us assume that your sitter has arrived and is sitting there because they are in the Job Market and have that morning received three job offers in the mail. They are uncertain of which to take. The financial packages, perks, etc., are all equal so there is no way to decide by viewing these aspects of the offers.

Get your sitter to number their options silently in their mind. Take Company 1, take Company 2, take Company 3, for example. You don't want to know which is which. Then get them to add a fourth option; Do nothing. Your sitter is basing their question on the situation as they see it at that moment in time; there may be some facts that they may not have heard of yet, but, possibly will in the not too distant future. Let them arrange things in their mind then shuffle the double pack until they are satisfied with the feel as before. Cards back to you, you lay them out as in Diagram 7.

Note : You do not read any of the cards in this spread.

You are simply laying them out to get an indication of the Path, not the influences. It will be fairly obvious as we go along as to why it would be confusing to try and read them. You know there are four options so you lay out four cards (Cards 1, 2, 3 and 4) showing the present situation in regard to each option. Under these you lay Cards 5, 6, 7 and 8 which equate to each of the four options in 3 months time. Each line of cards after that represents a further 3 months progression in that particular option. You continue to lay them out across the spread until you see a duplication.

In our Diagram the first we would see would be Card 16 duplicating Card 4. In this instance what is being indicated is the fact that the indicated influence would be back again 9 months time and the sitter will begin to cycle through the influences of Cards 4, 8, 12 and 16 until they make some further drastic change to their lives. Suggest that Option Four is disregarded and carry on with the other three; ignoring any further Work with Option Four - it is dead.

As you lay Card 19 under Option Three you see that it is a duplication of Card 10 in Option Two. What the Cards are saying is that in 1 year's time the situation will be the same in Option Three as it would have been in Option Two after only 6 months. Selecting Option Three would add a further six months in time to the situation, therefore consider Option Three as no longer being viable and continue to lay cards on Options One and Two.

Laying Card 22 at the 18 month level you spot that it is a duplicate of Card 14 in Option Two at the 9 month level, therefore following Option One would add a further 9 months to achieve a certain situation. This would preclude following Option One and leave Option Two as the only viable course of action to take.

Although it is not necessary, you can, if you wish, then read the Cards in the final Option, but it is suggested that you do not go beyond the last card, Card 21. However, remember that we have said that you should not read beyond three months since the number of variables would be coming excessive and can not offer either a true or accurate picture of the then situation. Cards 10, 14, 18 and 21 are pushing possibilities to extremes.

Remember Discrimination in using this particular spread.

In the final chat, after the tape has been stopped, whilst the 'energy exchange' takes place and you're getting ready to ease them out, rewind the tape for your sitter so that it is ready for them to play again when they are ready. It is a courteous gesture.

Also advise the sitter that the contents of the tape are very personal to them. It is their decision if they want to play it to anybody else; which could bring a mixed reaction from others. The only proviso to make to this is in regard to the spouse or 'marriage partner', as long as they are sympathetic to the Tarot or other things. Let them hear it because, being so close, they are going to be effected by the influences about the sitter as well. But, always leave it to the discretion and choice of the sitter; they know their partner, you don't.

Finally, there any number of spreads that you can use. A wander through the library will show you many books on the Tarot and all will list a few different spreads. Some huge, some small. Scan them through and see what attracts you. Try them out on your own, without too much attention being paid to the decode, other than the definitions of the placements. As you become more and more attuned to the Tarot you may well devise your own spread. Sure, the Tarot is a serious metaphysical tool and used wisely can be of great benefit both to yourself and to others, but, as with all things, find the Joy in what you are doing and do it well. Have fun.

Chapter 9

The Secret Tarot

Whilst we are looking at the Tarot I thought it might be helpful to let you into the secrets of some of the lesser known Workings of the Pack.

Towards the end of the 1980's I took some time out and went to listen to an evening lecture on Numerology. Fascinating, but I've always had a problems with maths and sums. Besides which there was a tremendous amount of knowledge that one needed to learn. Pages and pages of definitions of particular numbers, with a few hundred exceptions thrown in for good measure. Talk about brain ache.

Anyway, purely as a matter of interest, I sat with the calculator and started to look at my own details. I finished up with a page or so of numbers with absolutely no idea of the decode. I put it all away and forgot about it. The Merlin slipped in one day, soon after, and whispered in my ear words to the effect of taking all numbers to less than 22 and look at the Tarot. He then disappeared and left me to it. Whilst I may not be the quickest in the mental Olympics, it didn't take me too long to get his drift. Equate the final number with the cards of the Major Arcana.

To present my findings, we have to revert to my interpretations of each card, and give a brief resume of my views of the people the cards represent, then I can demonstrate how to use it.

First off, we can forget 0, the Fool, because no final number will ever end up with it and anyway we are always the Fool journeying through life's lessons.

Out first card, therefore, is 1, The Magician. A wheeler-dealer, manipulator of people and situations to whatever end; not necessarily as negative as it might seem to imply. Someone who is approached to get things sorted. A trouble shooter, on occasions.

The second is obviously 2, The High Priestess. A person who holds a great deal of Wisdom, probably unwittingly. Drawing on unknown depths of experience. Someone others seem to automatically turn to in order to talk things out to find a solution to their problems.

Next we have 3, The Empress. Very much the Mother figure in all respects; caring for and nurturing those to whom there is a sense of responsibility. However in the concept of pregnancy there is a slight tendency towards requiring another to stimulate actions to fruition.

4, The Emperor, is strength personified as in the concepts of the Father and the commander and controller of situations. Someone who sets the rules, lives by them and expects others to do the same. A firm and trusted ally in times of need.

5, The Hierophant, is enigmatic. This person seems to coexist in many places at once. For instance, they blend with any environment and appear to be at home wherever they are. Has an equal foot in opposing worlds; such as a steady foot in the physical, but the other foot is equally stable in the spiritual or other realms.

6, The Lovers, requires me to wax philosophical in order to clarify the concept behind this card. The philosophy maintains that when a person was in spirit before incarnation, they undertook to undergo certain, specified experiences in order to evolve spiritually. The geography of the place of birth and the parents were chosen with this long term view in mind. The geography is necessary in order to be born into the system that gives a social context in which to work. The parents are chosen in order to give the upbringing and necessary discipline, or lack of it, to the child in order to prepare it for the lessons of adulthood. It has been said that this choice also includes the date and time of birth, plus the date, time and method of departure. The problem is that, when we are born, we tend to forget why we are here and discover that we've left our notes behind. If you can accept the idea of this philosophy, when you are up to your neck in the brown and smelly (manure), just remember that you chose this. Don't blame anybody else but yourself. Take comfort in the fact that your are learning something you need to learn in the longer view. To get back to the cards, anyone with this particular number vibration tends to be those to whom things 'happen', and, no matter what they do, they are always in some sort of 'problem' area. They appear to lurch from crisis to crisis.

7, The Chariot, is all about movement. The world's perpetual nomads. They may settle somewhere, but will soon have itchy feet and feel compelled to move on to pastures new all the time. They never stay in one place for very long. A year or two and they're off again.

8, Strength. Whatever these types do, they are the mainstay of it. Solid, dependable, perhaps sometimes unimaginative. Often quiet natured, but not always. The copers of the world, who appear to deal with whatever crosses their path with hardly the bat of an eyelid.

The Hermit, 9, are those who just don't get involved. They tend to be the watchers in regard to what everyone else is doing. They are not, however, the wall-flowers of life. They stand and watch because they prefer things that way. If you can get close enough to them you will find that they have a tremendous depth of knowledge upon which to draw in order to advise you in any given situation because they have seen it all happen before.

10, Wheel of Fortune. If life was a fairground, these people would be on the white knuckle roller coaster all the time. Their lives continuously climb and plunge to extremes. In general terms, no matter how hard they work towards a goal, once they have achieved it they seem to quickly lose it and begin on something else. Up one minute, down the next.

11, Justice. Hard people to accept. They know what is right or wrong for them, however they have a slight tendency toward imposing their rules on others. Unlike the figure of Justice in the judicial system, this figure is not blindfolded. These people make their own judgement based on all the facts to hand. If they are aware that they don't have all the facts they tend to keep quiet and wait for further information. Rarely opinionated in their speech unless they are at least one hundred percent certain of what they are saying, they can however be quick to acknowledge anothers superior information and withdraw from the argument until they have sifted and checked the new information for themselves, reforming their opinions in the light of this if it appears necessary.

12, The Hanged Man. Life's go-fors. These people seem to end up doing everything for everybody else and achieve little for themselves, but they do find a great deal of personal satisfaction in this way. They tend to be the willing carers in society.

13, Death. People who respond to this vibration are in a constant state of flux. Everything is about change. Death and Rebirth. The end of one thing and the beginning of something new, but not as erratic as the grass-hopper. Each change is a growth experience.

14, Temperance. These people are an essential part of the stable element in any society. They keep their feet firmly on the ground, but they do allow their heads to drift in the clouds, however all the while they recognise the practicalities of Life and don't get carried away with apparently futile dreams.

15, The Devil. Materialists. Pragmatists. If they can't see it, feel it, fight it, bite it, etc., then it doesn't exist. Totally locked into the physical world with little or no imagination. They can lay plans, but they've got to be practical plans. No castles in the skies for these people unless there is the science to support such a concept, for example, sustained levitation through the use of electromagnets or similar.

16, The Tower. Everything seems to happen to these people. They are interesting to be around. Bolts come out of the blue from every angle and keep these people on the hop. They have few dull moments. They may just have time to drag in a quick breath before they are off again on some journey or adventure through life.

Tarot 17, The Star. The card of the Dreamers. The Visionaries. Their eyes see beyond normal sight. They dream great dreams, but are they capable of Dancing the Dream-time Awake? Unfortunately, few are. Those who do manage it make an impact on their environment and are held in esteem by their peers.

18, The Moon. Followers of Destiny. Their lives appear to have been pre-ordained and they follow it religiously. They walk their Yellow Brick Road unstintingly. Learning and growing all the while. Accepting whatever happens to them.

19, The Sun. The Free-wheelers. Those who seem to have no end of options open to them. Whatever they want to do, they seem to be able to get on and do it. Obstacles for lesser mortals just seem to drop away.

20, Judgement. Another hard type of person to be around. As the card implies, judgmental. Their saving grace, however, is that the majority of their judgements are about themselves. These judgements can be taken to extremes however. They are not nearly as good as anybody else and they are always putting themselves down. In the other extreme, they can be somewhat bigoted in their regard to others, always finding fault and with few kind words. To find the happy medium is very difficult for these people.

21, The World. Our last card. My understanding of this card within a Tarot reading is that a new opportunity is opening shortly; a whole new ball game. This carries over into the type casting of these individuals. For them fresh opportunities are a constant factor in their lives, which they can elect to follow or not as they decide. Confident in the knowledge that if one fails, there will be another in the fullness of time.

I've gone through the decode, now, how do you get the code in the first place? It is a very simple exercise. Take and transpose each letter into a number, then add all the numbers together to arrive at a final number, from which you can go to our decode list above. The method of this comes from the little table shown below :

1	2	3	4	5	6	7	8	9
A	B	C	D	E	F	G	H	I
J	K	L	M	N	O	P	Q	R
S	T	U	V	W	X	Y	Z	

Without involving anybody else in this and infringing their privacy I am forced to offer myself as the guinea pig in explaining how this works, so please bear with me. Let us take my first name of Geoff and show you the numerical equivalent.

G is 7; E is 5; O is 6; F is 6; F is 6. Add the 7, 5, 6, 6, and 6 together to get 30. Now, as The Merlin suggested, earlier, we have to bring it down to less than 22, therefore we add the 3 and the 0 to give us a final number of 3. Refer to the decode in the previous pages and you can see the vibration that runs with the card that equates to the number 3. Easy? Of course it is. If it wasn't I couldn't do it.

My full name of Geoffrey Howard Hughes (my parents had a sense of humour) works out as Geoffrey, 7; 5; 6; 6; 6; 9; 5; 7, which adds up to 51. Howard is 8; 6; 5; 1; 9; 4, giving 33. Hughes is 8; 3; 7; 8; 5; 1, which give us a 32. We then take these three numbers, 51; 33; 32, and add them all together to get a final number, which is 116. Too big, so reduce to a number less than 22 by adding each of them together, which equals 8. This shows the vibration that your parents wished upon you; their dream for you. Don't get upset if you feel they have done you a disfavour. They haven't. Bear in mind that they probably didn't know about this sort of thing, and remember the philosophy of The Lovers. How often are you actually referred to by your full name? I'll bet its not very often. The Full Name Vibration is only one of many influences that you carry with you.

For instance if like me you were baptised, you were named by your forenames into the church, ignoring your surname. Therefore for me I was named Geoffrey Howard. Taking these two words we can get an idea of the Religious Vibration that will have an effect upon us. Mine comes down to 84 which is a 12.

Okay, you've got the swing of it now, so lets have a look at what you can do with it, now that you have seen how it works. By the by, you may remember the eccentric multi-millionaire, Howard Hughes? It comes down to 65, which is 11. See above and form your own conclusions as to whether this is a viable system to work with. We have got the full name but, as suggested above you don't actually run under that in Life, unless you use it in your signature. The Signature Vibration. I have two signatures. A 'Bank' one and another semi-official one. The 'Bank' Signature spells out Geoffrey H Hughes which is 91, giving a 10; reflecting my chequing account very accurately. The semi-official is just G Hughes, which gives us a 39, which is 12. Personal mail goes out as Geoff (3) or Geoff Hughes (62 = 8), whilst notes, etc., go out with a simple G (7). This appendage to a letter indicates the vibration that you are radiating to the recipient.

Before we move on from names let us have a look at those names that other people call us, or, at least, the printable ones. Much to my embarrassment many people refer to me as either Merlin (8), or The Merlin (5). It is how they see me; not my conscious radiation I might add. Between June (5) and I the words 'sweetheart' (7), 'love' (9) and 'darling' (9) get used quite often. In a Magical Working situation I invariably refer to her as either 'Priestess' (5) or 'My Lady' (8).

Which brings us to Appointment Vibrations and Title Vibrations. In the UK I live under a monarchy headed currently by The Queen (5), referring to her as either 'Her Majesty' (7). or 'Your Majesty' (10). Well known personages, for instance, such as Prince Charles (11), or Charles (9), is The Prince of Wales (8). I hear that in the United States of America he is known as Chuck (10). His estranged wife, formerly Lady Diana Spencer (7), now, officially, Diana, Princess of Wales (13), commonly referred to as Di (13).

How about The President (8), Mr President (6), or Mister President (5)? What will be the result when a woman is elected as President? Madame President (7), Mrs President (7) or Ms President (7)? Remember how we would refer to JFK (9)? Nixon (4)? Clinton (6)? The title of President often being dropped. Indicative of the level of esteem held by the talker for the person they are talking about.

To us lesser mortals.

My Secretary (8). The Accountant (8). The Boss (7). Housewife (12). Environmental Domestic Engineer (15). Mother (7). Mom (14). Father (4). Dad (9). Pop (20). Check your own Job Description and see how the company view your position. Remember the Pet Names and such that are thrown around between family and friends. What do they tell you? How does one person view another?

Moving on, we come to the Life Path Vibration. Check out your Birthdate. Use the simple data involved in the number of the month through the year. January is 1, February is 2, and so on. Don't forget the 19'. My birthdate is January 14, 1943. Adding each number separately we come to 23, which comes down to 5. Year Vibration. With a little bit of thought you can soon see what a particular year is all about. 1995, for instance, carried an overall vibration of 6, whilst 1996 had a 7, and 1997 will be an 8. You can also check out your Personal Year Vibration by taking the actual date of your birthday in a particular year. January 14, 1995, showed the year up to my next birthday was on a vibration of 3, whilst in 1996 it was a 4, and 1997 will be a 5.

The Environmental Vibration can also be determined. Take your house number, road, town or city name, county or state and the postal code and add them all together. Our address came down to 15, but we dropped the house number and named the house Avallon, which gave us a 14. Shortly thereafter we became aware of a subtle change in the way our home runs and other people's perception of our home. Thinking of moving house? Check the address to get an idea of the sort of harmonic you can expect if you live there. Working? Check out the full address of your company. What is the vibration there? Job hunting? Check the position title and the address of where you are considering working. Do you want to be in that sort of vibration?

How about your Telephone Vibration? Add all the National Dial Code to the actual number to see what you get. We have discovered that anyone ending up with a 12 has relatively high bills. Ours comes down to a 5, which we are content with. How about your office number or extension number? What about International Calls? Telephoning family, friends or businesses in other countries? Check exactly what you are dialling and this will give you an indication of how you feel about the people or organisation you are making contact with. How about your car? Check the licence plate. Check the make and model as well. 12s, in my experience, have a tendency to be expensive to run and maintain. Many of the above you can take steps to change if you so wish; but bear in mind the philosophy of The Lovers card.

Don't become a slave to this, nor any other system. Life is about having fun and enjoying everything you do, so laugh on.

I can well recall one of the very first bits of magic that I sought to undertake; back in the 1970s. This was in the days long before I was Initiated and met The Merlin so I was acting very much on gut reactions. I had set up the room I was in to become a Lodge. I put a bowl of water in West, a candle burning in the East, a lighted incense stick in the South and a potted plant in the North. Each item representing one of the four elements. Some time had been spent with my, then, Marseilles Tarot and the little booklet, choosing cards which I considered to be helpful to what I was doing. I took all these cards, divided them into four piles and then placed them, one by one, around in a circle, joining the four cardinal points.

The magic was Worked within that apparently safe and secure area. It Worked and things proceeded in the desired direction; even if it didn't happen the way I had intended. Magic has a tendency to be like that. You set up the aim, fire up the magic and expect certain things to happen. Invariably they don't, but you do arrive at the target in the longer term.

Was the Tarot an integral part of the magic? Was it just a confidence booster? Who knows? I certainly cannot say for sure. Maybe it was both. If you're into magic, give it a whirl to find out, but also give some careful thought and consideration to the aims of your Working and which of the cards will be helpful or otherwise.

Talking of help reminds me of something else that you might find as a useful bit of trivia. Getting into the swing of my Earth Healing Work I discovered that whenever I set a date for a Working I was looking to the Full Moon. Whenever The Merlin, or someone similar, suggested a date for a Working that they wished me to carry through it was always without fail on or about the Dark or New Moon. This bothered me for some time until I was told of the magical reason. View the Moon Cycle as a triangle with the Dark of Moon at both lower ends of an upward pointing triangle and the Full Moon at the apex. Any Working carried out between the Dark and Full Moon would 'ride' the Moon Current to its apex of the Full Moon and off into the 'higher realms', much like using a launch ramp. Any Working carried out between the Full Moon and the Dark of Moon would 'ride' the Moon Current down to the Earth and 'crash', going nowhere. If you wish to bring something to its conclusion, then Work during the Full, Dark period. If you're looking to start something, then aim for the Dark to Full period.

Having begun my association with The Merlin I found myself doing various Workings on behalf of my Land and the Planet; making good the damage caused by Man. He had set me a particular task and the date had been set some weeks in advance. As I had tried to gather together the necessary people that we would need and decide on how we would all Work together to achieve the National Healing, I had found myself running around in circles for some time; trying this, trying that, in my mind. Nothing seemed to feel right.

Suddenly one evening just after the sun had set the penny had dropped and I saw exactly how it was meant to be Worked. Making my notes in my Diary I discovered that we were 22 days away from the set date. Obviously this reminded me of the Major

Arcana. I thought of the day of the Working to be 1, The Magician and considered that we were possibly working backwards through the Major Arcana and that the ideas for the Rite had come during the day of 0, The Fool. But it had come after sundown. Perhaps the changeover point was at that time, rather than midnight or dawn. In later years I was to learn of the Pagan Concept of the New Year beginning with the coming of the Winter, plus Shakespear's statement 'as the day follows night'; which seemed, in my mind, to validate the sundown theory.

At that time I decided to let it run, keep a note of it, and see what happened. It is now many years later and it still holds true for me. Additionally many others that I have met have also taken it up and as far as I am aware it still holds true for them. Once it is set up it is very simple to operate. I include a Chart of the dates of the day of The Fool, but ask you to bear in mind that it starts at sundown the previous day and changes to 21, The World, at sundown on the day shown. These dates were plotted from an Ephemera which shows the dates up to December 31, 2000, but what of after that? The inspiration came to look back through this century to find a year where January 1 would be a Monday and the preceding year would be a Leap Year. 1916 was just such a Leap Year and January 1, 1917, was a Monday.

With an understanding of the Major Arcana it should not be very long before you are able to see it Working, or otherwise, for you.

The Tarot Calendar Chart

1996	1997	1998	1999	2000	2001
Mon Jan 22	Wed Jan 8	Sat Jan 17	Mon Jan 4	Thu Jan 13	Sun Jan 21
Tue Feb 13	Thu Jan 30	Sun Feb 8	Tue Jan 26	Fri Feb 4	Mon Feb 12
Wed Mar 6	Fri Feb 21	Mon Mar 2	Wed Feb 17	Sat Feb 26	Tue Mar 6
Thu Mar 28	Sat Mar 15	Tue Mar 24	Thu Mar 11	Sun Mar 19	Wed Mar 28
Fri Apr 19	Sun Apr 6	Wed Apr 15	Fri Apr 2	Mon Apr 10	Thu Apr 19
Sat May 11	Mon Apr 28	Thu May 7	Sat Apr 24	Tue May 2	Fri May 11
Sun Jun 2	Tue May 20	Fri May 29	Sun May 16	Wed May 24	Sat Jun 2
Mon Jun 24	Wed Jun 11	Sat Jun 20	Mon Jun 8	Thu Jun 15	Sun Jun 24
Tue Jul 16	Thu Jul 3	Sun Jul 12	Tue Jun 29	Fri Jul 7	Mon Jul 16
Wed Aug 7	Fri Jul 25	Mon Aug 3	Wed Jul 21	Sat Jul 29	Tue Aug 7
Thu Aug 29	Sat Aug 16	Tue Aug 25	Thu Aug 12	Sun Aug 20	Wed Aug 29
Fri Sep 20	Sun Sep 7	Wed Sep 16	Fri Sep 3	Mon Sep 11	Thu Sep 20
Sat Oct 12	Mon Sep 29	Thu Oct 8	Sat Sep 25	Tue Oct 3	Fri Oct 12
Sun Nov 3	Tue Oct 21	Fri Oct 30	Sun Oct 17	Wed Oct 25	Sat Nov 3
Mon Nov 25	Wed Nov 12	Sat Nov 21	Mon Nov 8	Thu Nov 16	Sun Nov 25
Tue Dec 17	Thu Dec 4	Fri Dec 13	Tue Nov 30	Fri Dec 8	Mon Dec 17
		Fri Dec 26		Wed Dec 22	Sat Dec 30

2002	2003	2004	2005
Tue Jan 8	Fri Jan 17	Sun Jan 4	Wed Jan 12
Wed Jan 30	Sat Feb 8	Mon Jan 26	Thu Feb 3
Thu Feb 21	Sun Mar 2	Tue Feb 17	Fri Feb 25
Fri Mar 15	Mon Mar 24	Wed Mar 10	Sat Mar 19
Sat Apr 6	Tue Apr 15	Thu Mar 31	Sun Apr 10
Sun Apr 28	Wed May 7	Fri Apr 23	Mon May 2
Mon May 20	Thu May 29	Sat May 15	Tue May 24
Tue Jun 11	Fri Jun 20	Sun Jun 6	Wed Jun 15
Wed Jul 3	Sat Jul 12	Mon Jun 28	Thu Jul 7
Thu Jul 25	Sun Aug 3	Tue Jul 20	Fri Jul 29
Fri Aug 16	Mon Aug 25	Wed Aug 11	Sat Aug 20
Sat Sep 7	Tue Sep 16	Thu Sep 2	Sun Sep 11
Sun Sep 29	Wed Oct 8	Fri Sep 24	Mon Oct 3
Mon Oct 21	Thu Oct 30	Sat Oct 16	Tue Oct 25
Tue Nov 12	Fri Nov 21	Sun Nov 7	Wed Nov 16
Wed Dec 4	Sat Dec 13	Mon Nov 29	Thu Dec 8
Thu Dec 26		Sat Dec 21	Fri Dec 30

Chapter 10

Working With Crystal

You may well have noticed how, over the last decade or so, there seems to have been a spread of interest in Crystal. Homes and offices are sporting all manner of pieces of these beautiful lumps of rock. Not just as ornaments but also to refract the incoming sunlight and send a cascade of rainbows about the room. Referring you back to our very first chapter and looking at our heritage it may seem to indicate a legendary affinity between people and crystals. It has been suggested that with the Change of Age that seems to be coming in and in the alteration of various energies world-wide, that many of the ancient Atlanteans are coming back into incarnation and are bringing within them an understanding of the many facets of crystal energy. Unfortunately there are very few who actually remember the properties of the crystal, and what it can and cannot do, along with the correct usage of such energy.

When The Merlin and I first got together I soon gravitated towards Working with the bits of crystal that came into my possession. He got me to have a very brief look at what crystal is. According to my smaller dictionary it is quartz, and an 'aggregation of molecules with definite internal structure and external form of solid enclosed by symmetrically arranged plane faces'. I turned to the listing under quartz and found 'kinds of mineral, massive or crystallising in hexagonal prisms, consisting in pure form of silica or silicon dioxide'. I didn't find any of that too helpful so spent some time sitting and communing with my crystals; with just the odd kick from The Merlin when I was going walk-about inside my head.

As mentioned in our first few pages, the Atlanteans used crystal as a transmitter of energies between various points and, thus, the whole of their economy was based on crystal energy. They were totally dependent upon it. Hang on a minute! Back to those dictionary definitions; '... pure form of silica or silicon dioxide'. Whilst our economy may be based on petro-chemicals, what actually controls those same items? The many and varied forms of computers transmit and receive the instructive information. What do we have in the computer? A Central Processing Unit, and in the heart of that there is at least one silicon chip. Without that little bit of crystal the whole thing would just be so much scrap iron. Are we back to, in reality, a crystal based economy? How many times have you phoned a company with a problem and, after much discussion, often quite heated, been silenced by being told that they cannot do that because the computer wont accept it. Infuriating isn't it? As an aside, the computer will do whatever we tell it to do, no fuss; its just that the programmers have failed to allow for some variations. This is not the fault of the computer; the blame lies with the programmer. Truly do people say GIGO - garbage in, garbage out.

Back to our crystals. Under The Merlin's prodding I came to the conclusion that crystal is a physical element of Earth that has been subjected to tremendous heat and pressure by the surrounding strata and formed quartz. Such quartz, depending on the other minerals in the area, takes on various colours and are then referred to as particular types of quartz crystal. For instance, amethyst, and rose quartz. There is an extensive list of the various names that mankind has given them, but they are all, basically, quartz crystal. The intrusion of some other mineral fused within them does not alter the major property, it just adds a harmonic, which leads us to say such things as rose quartz being a very strong pacifier.

Science has found that if you pass an electric current through a coil of wire which is passed around a crystal, the crystal will vibrate; which is where we get the piezo-electric effect which lies at the heart of many cigarette lighters and quartz watches.

The Merlin advised that raw crystal is an accumulator for a natural free-flowing energy that surrounds us all. It collects the energy within itself and then releases it from its point in a needle like projection. A natural radiation. All quite normal. Until, that is, somebody comes along and rips the crystal from it's natural place within the Earth. The ripping free 'stuns' the crystal and the 'shock' turns the crystal 'off'. It is no longer capable of transmitting it's natural energy. In the vast majority of instances all those pieces of crystal scattered around rooms supposedly beaming 'energy' to all and sundry are, in fact, as dead as a door-nail. Any belief in such happenings is pure fantasy; borne in the minds of those who dream on.

In a few cases, however, where individual people have attained a substantial rapport with the crystals, they can be turned 'on' again by those same people. Establish a rapport? There may well be many ways, but I know of only one and will set that down for you to have a play with. Get hold of a piece of raw quartz, preferably approximately half an inch in diameter and no more than an inch or two in length, with a natural point on one end. When I stipulate raw, I mean unpolished and uncut except for the cut where it was actually taken from the Earth.

Place this quartz against your sternum (the connecting bone at the front of your rib-cage) and sing. Yes, sing. Sing anything you like, it doesn't matter what sort of song it is and you certainly don't have to be anything but a bath-tub songster. Don't worry about the words, lah-lah Works just as well; even humming a tune will Work.

It is suggested that ladies may get on with their work or chores with the crystal held securely in their bra' whilst gentlemen could try a piece of sticking plaster - just be careful when you peel it off.

As you sing-along you should find that whenever you hit a certain note, or notes, the crystal will vibrate against you. Spend some time identifying these notes and sing them alone to check them out. One will, eventually, prove to bring a deeper response than the others. Concentrate on that one. Spend a little time on it until you can be sure that you can go straight to the note and get a response, then stop. Take a few deep breathes, relax, and then sing that one note as gently as possible and for as long as you can.

Don't force it. If you find that you haven't quite got it right, just slip either side of the starting note until you feel a very positive response and hold on to that one. You will know, beyond any shadow of doubt, when it is right, I assure you, because not only will the crystal resonate as before, but will begin to amplify it as well. Don't be alarmed, this feeling is perfectly natural and, as you Work with it, you will find it both pleasant and relaxing. Your sternum will pick up this vibration and transmit it, and, in due course, will set the whole of your skeletal structure vibrating in sympathy. It is truly amazing.

Those of you that have read Anne McCaffrey's *Crystal Singer* might now understand what she meant when she spoke of the Singers losing all sense of time and becoming enthralled by the crystal song. Here, obviously, is the warning. Don't become over-enamoured of singing crystal.

Okay, you've got the note, now forget the singing for a little while. You have stimulated that particular piece of crystal back into action. Now check it out for yourself to see that you have. Remove the crystal from your chest - gentlemen, carefully. Take the crystal in your active hand (right if right handed; left if left handed) with the single point upper-most. Cup your passive hand (the other one) over the top of the point, about half and inch above it. Let this hand go soft; very relaxed and gentle, back to stroking a bubble without bursting it.

Lazily, gently, let your cupped hand slide from side to side, keeping the point underneath it. Assuming you are nice and relaxed you should feel a small, blunt point of energy crossing your palm in line with the point. Some feel it as heat, others as coldness, others as a tingling. What you are feeling is the accumulated and triggered amplification of raw power by the crystal into a totally benign jet of energy.

As we have travelled and demonstrated these abilities both June and I have noticed that, for some unknown and totally inexplicable reason ladies who are menstruating tend not to be able to feel the energies on their palms. Baffling.

I even came to discover that merely thinking of the note in my mind would set the crystals Working, and it is equally possible to 'think' the crystal into silence. They can be switched on or off at will.

As I Worked with The Merlin and he led me towards Earth Healing he got me to using four small pieces of amethyst which were positioned in such a way that they were directing their energies to another larger piece of amethyst which was positioned with its point pointing down towards the Earth. The streams of energy were coming from the small pieces into the larger, enhancing its own energy stream, and burning its way down into the Earth; bringing a Healing Energy to the Planet. There will be a lot more about that towards the end of these pages. Interestingly, over a period of time, the amethyst colour drained from the crystals and I was left with five pieces of clear crystal.

I began to experiment with these Crystal Energies and looked towards the healing abilities as far as healing people is concerned. Like many others I experimented upon myself. Set the energy running and directed the power flows into myself. I have a prolapsed disc or two in my lower back which can be extremely painful at times. I was looking to using these energies as a measure of calming the inflammation and allowing myself to get around with some modicum of comfort. A few nights later I was awoken by excruciating pains in my left, rear side. I had Mount Everest inside me. Drinks came back the wrong way. I rolled around the bed in agony. The Doctor was summoned, a sedative administered for what was left of the night, and I was admitted to hospital the next morning and placed on a drip. It was diagnosed as a Kidney Stone, which had lodged and was blocking the natural outlet. A deft anal prod by the doctor shifted the Stone and I was able to relax and recuperate. I was eventually discharged from hospital with the stern instruction to drink at least three litres of water a day in the hope of flushing it out. I went into the regime and, some little while later, something rattled around the toilet pan. I fished it out and had a look.

It measured approximately one sixteenth of an inch by an eighth of an inch and was entirely made of tiny pieces of crystal which had fused together. In the wrong place it had felt huge. As I pondered on this I came to the personal conclusion that, somehow, the crystal energy I had been using on myself had caused the microscopic flakes of crystal that naturally exist in my body and blood stream had, somehow, become attracted to each other, welded themselves together and had formed the 'rock' that had got into my kidney.

I began to realise the affinity between my body and that of crystal. I got to experimenting on myself. I sang to 'me'. Sure enough, there is a certain note that sets my skeletal frame-work resonating exactly the same as the other note would set the crystal vibrating. This got me to thinking. If my body and crystal Worked the same, why did I need crystal at all? Experiments were undertaken. I ended up with the findings that if I pointed my finger and 'thought sang' my note, a beam of energy would leave the tip and beam across the room. Demonstrating this to students in our workshops has brought confirmation from them that the two energies are exactly the same. Now I know why I was told that it was rude to point.

Sitting in one of those idle moments, mind in neutral, information began to trickle in. Under the surface of the planet there are millions of crystal caves. The ceilings, walls and floors packed with crystal points orientated in every conceivable direction. They are all switched 'on' since no-one has torn them from the living rock. Their beams of energy are permeating every inch of the planet beneath our feet. The realisation came that they are there for some extremely important reason, which I do not truly understand, except through conjecture as to the possibility of them being a form of energy life-blood of the Earth. They are a part of the mechanism of the planet. I sincerely believe that they should remain in the Earth.

Whilst we do have pieces of crystal in our home, we no longer collect them as we did before. I beg you to consider leaving them in the Earth to do their Work, please.

Chapter 11

Geophysical Changes & Extra Terrestrials

There is much speculation, throughout the World, about all sorts of planetary changes that are supposedly going to happen in the not too distant future. There is at least one organisation that I know of in the United States of America that has even produced a continental map of North America as it is anticipated to be by the year 2000. The whole of the East coast under the Atlantic, the Great Lakes combined into one, the Mississippi connecting that single lake to the Gulf of Mexico, the Appalachian Mountains forming a separate land mass, California and some areas of the surrounding States under the Pacific.

In a conversation with The Merlin many, many years ago in regard to Great Britain, he did advise me that 'Norfolk and The Fens' would return to the sea. No matter how often I questioned him I could not get any idea of a time scale. When circumstances forced June and I to move to live in Norfolk I must admit that I did go into a bit of a panic and a lot of abuse winged its way upstairs. Remember, I'm a devout coward. But things have happened since we have moved here.

Back in 1990, before June and I got together, Working with a very small group of people I had found myself in contact with a pair of energies that we came to know as Cheiron and Chyeimea. Much as I did when I was Working with The Merlin on the Release of the Pendragon Energy (see *Ancient Magicks for a New Age*) I went onto a three day cycle for channelling information from these two energies. That is, day one would be where I actually channelled, day two would be where I would then transcribe the information from the tapes recorded, and ostensibly day three was a day off to rest. It didn't Work quite like that, but we got there in the end.

This lasted for three solid months; from the Summer Solstice to the Autumn Equinox. No matter where I was in the country, or what we were doing, we sat with the recorder turned on.

With the actual information received and the resulting brain juggling trying to understand what we were being told, we ended up with over a hundred hours on tape, which came down to close on three thousand pages of close typing. Much of which is still not understood, but one day it will be. During that time we also became involved in various Workings in regard to certain geophysical changes; mainly along major earth energy lines. We were constantly afraid, I admit, of the results of what we were doing. It is now self evident that our fears were groundless because none of the physical changes appear to have taken place. But we still had to sweat it out at the time.

If we look back in history, there has always been some kind of furore running about the coming of Armageddon and the end of the World. It is also evident from watching the metaphysical press now that some of the changes that were orchestrated by other entities in other realms have taken effect in the sense of different energy vibrations permeating the world. People's awareness seems to be changing. In the short term the weather appears to be acting up out of the normal seasonal averages.

At the same time as we were Working on these changes we noticed that, in Britain, the numbers of crop circles suddenly became big news. The popular press exploded with photographs and pundits trotted out all sorts of ideas and theories. Books were published and people scrabbled for information. I was the same. However, being on a trip in Southern England at the time, I was privileged to come across a new circle, less than 24 hours old. I wandered in, asking permission of the Guardian of Place (see *Seasonal Rites*, Chapter 13) and went and laid in the centre of it. I put up a polite query and the following information trickled in.

The circles were being generated by off world energies and the sole purpose of the circles was to make people think. The shapes, designs and such like were irrelevant. Any correspondence with known hieroglyphs was purely co-incidental.

I left and came into contact with many other people who had undergone experiences in their awareness of the circles. No-one else had anything like the information I had received. One lecturer had stated that in his understanding of the designs within 5 years we would lose electricity. I'm writing this in 1996 on my PC. It would seem it hasn't been lost yet.

The same belief is still floating around, however. Only last night in a telephone conversation we heard that the Earth is entering some sort of photon belt and that as we get deeper into it so electricity will disappear. (My preview reader, Stuart Allison - affectionately known as Vlad of the Red Pen - has a scientific bent and advises me that photons are light particles which do not come in belts and they stream out of the sun all of the time and obviously we still have electricity.) As far as I am aware, scientists still don't fully understand very much about electricity. Sure, we know how it works and what it does, but we don't know why.

Getting back to the circles, the press made a great splash of the fact that a couple of men had admitted to creating a circle or two one night. They had said that it had seemed like a good idea at the time. Perhaps I am stretching things a bit, but if you would now take a moment or two and cast your mind back to the Contact Chapter, did we not say that the initial input that you would receive would be by way of Inspiration? Why couldn't this have been the same sort of thing? They were inspired? The circle had appeared and people had started thinking. Objective achieved. The other powers can be very sneaky in the way they get things done.

Having moved to Norfolk, June and I had begun our travels abroad. We had gone to Iceland and on a day in the ice and snow at a place called Thingvellir where I had been carrying out a small Working on behalf of the Icelandic Guardians, June had been startled to see clairvoyantly two beings step out from behind some rocks. In a subliminal conversation she had been advised that they were not spirits but extra-terrestrials who were residing in the area for a while. Subsequently as we moved around Iceland we both became aware of others who were also spending some time on our planet.

June was reminded of a vision she had one night. It appears that at some time in the long past an alien ship had visited Planet Earth and had been forced to leave some of the crew behind. It appears that they were of a different molecular structure to us and vibrated at a much higher rate which made them invisible to the naked eye. For some unexplained reason it was many, many years before a craft had returned to the planet and re-established contact with these ETs. They had taken refuge deep in the earth away from those of us on the surface. I feel this may be similar to the Star Trek Prime Directive; non-interference, non-contamination. Over the centuries these beings had followed their own course of evolution and now regarded the Earth as their home. They didn't want to leave when the crafts had returned. It seems that there is a whole world of beings deep within the molecular structure of the planet of which we are totally unaware except through clairvoyant flashes of obscure scenes.

Back in England we were introduced to a man who is very much into Unidentified Flying Objects. Through him, we took a long drive to listen to a lecture by a man named Sixto Paz, a Peruvian, who maintained that he had made contact with Extra-Terrestrials and even journeyed in one of their craft to Gannymede. In Earth time he had been away for about 15 minutes, but when he had stepped out to be reunited with his waiting friends, he had at least five days growth of beard on his normally clean shaven face. He talked on and I became more and more stunned. He was explaining, in slightly different words, exactly the same concepts that we had channelled back in 1990, or at least the ones we had finally understood. I had driven home in confusion and I lost three days as I pounded the carpet trying to get my mind in order. We had assumed that Cheiron and Chyeimea were spiritual entities. What if they weren't? What if they were Extra-Terrestrials? Had I been misled? Were we all being tricked?

What did this make of the Dragon and Moon Swords? Were they magical weapons for Earth healing or simply extra-terrestrial electrodes for the same reason? Much of the Cheiron Tapes had been introducing us to various subtle energies that are inherent in the Dragon Sword. This would explain why The Merlin had been insistent that having given me the initial Dragon Sword Energy I had to carry it wherever I went in the world. If it is an electrode then it would need to be inserted into the earth at the point where the off-world energy could be beamed from elsewhere into that particular spot and do its job. This would seem to indicate a logical explanation for its reality. However I am aware that once the two Swords have been to a specific location there is a form of 'psychic link' between them and that spot and they can continue their Work on that spot from anywhere else should it ever be required.

Having given my lectures on our Magical Quest and spoken of the many and varied energies that are about I always offered members of the audience the chance to hold one or other of the two Swords to feel for themselves. Putting my money where my mouth was. The people concerned have reacted to the touch in a variety of ways dependant entirely upon their own individuality. From deep emotional outbursts to a total sense of calmness. One or two have been so spaced that we have had to step in and bring them back to earth. Nearly everyone has reported a great sense of spiritual involvement: angels; archangels; the Light and so on. If these are simple ET electrodes how come others get that sort of response?

For ourselves, we have lived, breathed and Worked so closely with the two of them that we feel little or nothing from them. We know what's there to a degree and rarely go in to play with them.

After various telephone conversations reporting Sixto Paz' statements to others across the country, we came to the conclusion that it was the information that is important, not its manner of broadcasting. There had to be many, many people who wouldn't be seen dead in a Spiritual or Spiritualist environment, but would quite happily go to listen to a talk on U.F.O.s; and vice versa. The information is getting out.

121

One vital piece of information that we had tuned into dealt with the concept of time and distance that we have on our planet. By air the journey from London, England to Sydney, Australia takes somewhere in the region of thirty hours. Cheiron insisted that this is too long, they were looking for a time frame of four hours. He claimed that we already have the technology and it simply needs to be picked up and refined. Not so many years ago it used to take anything up to six weeks to complete the same journey. The World has, therefore, shrunk, but it needs to shrink a great deal more. Today, we have satellites beaming information instantaneously about the globe and the internet and e-mail linking person to person. We are, it would appear, gradually getting there. Perhaps the physical ability isn't so far into the future? We have to remember that it was less than a hundred years ago that Wilbur and Orville Wright made the first flight at Kittyhawk. Nowadays we have been to the Moon and things have gone even further into space. Where we will be able to get to tomorrow?

Robert Dean, an inactive (retired to us Brits) U.S. Marine Corps Command Sergeant Major, and a noted ufologist of many years standing has gone on record that he is beginning to turn from the idea of little green men and flying saucers as previously envisaged and is beginning to see a deeply religious or spiritual significance to these visitations, with the added conviction, in my interpretation of what he was saying, that perhaps these beings aren't aliens but facets of multi-dimensional beings such as ourselves. They aren't any different to us, they just operate in another dimension, much as we do when go into an altered state of consciousness.

Time went by and every now and again I would sit and mull over the ideas of the geophysical changes and the extra-terrestrials, becoming more and more confused. Until one day, after a spate of programmes on U.F.Os. via the satellite television I was, once again pondering. The mind was stimulated by the following input of information. When the space-craft are travelling through space they are at one vibrationary rate, but in order to enter the Earth's surface they have to downshift to another vibratory rate. It is whilst they are switching from one rate to the other that they become visible to us. Depending upon their change rate, so the craft becomes visible for seconds or minutes. The fact that certain areas of the world seem to report more sightings than others would seem to suggest that these were population centres for the earth-bound aliens.

Suddenly the whole idea of major geophysical changes happening overnight by the year 2000 struck me as totally ludicrous. Cheiron and many others had spent a great deal of time and energy impressing us of the need for the Earth to shrink. If the seas were to suddenly rise and engulf all the areas that I have outlined previously those on Earth would go into a very deep trauma. Towns and cities would mobilise whatever resources they could muster and become very insular, even if looking to others for assistance which probably wouldn't be forthcoming, since they would have their own problems to deal with.

With the likes of Texas and other oil producing areas disappearing overnight under the sea where would the petro-chemicals come from to power such machines as we have? Planes, boats, cars and so on. An hour's drive would become a thirteen and three quarter hour walk. The great ocean going liners would be without oil, therefore unable to go to sea. We would have to look back at the use of wind-power and, instead of taking six weeks to get from England to Australia, it would take months. Distances would increase to unimaginable proportions. No doubt we could look towards nuclear power or revert to fossil burning engines, but that would take time, perhaps a very long time. The giant electricity grids across the nations would be cut. Yes, the death of electricity to many areas.

I do not deny that the changes may well occur, but I just cannot see it happening in that way. If the seas were to gradually encroach onto the land, then we would be in a situation where we could gradually retrench; backing up in the face of the incoming tides. Since originally writing this paragraph we have spotted a couple of items on the television in regard to Norfolk and the Fens. The little seaside village of Happisburg perches on the North Norfolk Cliffs. Some miles to the East, on the edge of the Norfolk Broads at the tributary of the River Yare the local

123

officials are planning to spend millions of pounds on strengthening the sea defences to hold the North Sea out of the Broads. In Happisburg the cliffs are crumbling at a rate of some 30 feet per year, homes are being evacuated and left to tumble into the sea. The commentator commented that it would appear that the Sea was coming into the Broads by way of the back-door. It looks like we will have to back up in order that we will be able to preserve our resources and civilisation, as we currently know it, would continue and evolve.

That is always assuming, of course, that the ETs don't step in, in some manner.

A couple of little anecdotes to finish this chapter and give you something else to think about.

The mother of a friend passed to spirit in December, '95. She came through to visit her daughter via June. As the chatter was coming to an end I asked permission for a question. This was agreed. I simply asked if she was 'spooky' or extra-terrestrial? Her reply : *"For the moment I am spooky, but in my Father's house there are many mansions. You won't truly understand until you get here."*

A little while later a visiting spirit was questioned if he could fix it for me to meet an ET. He replied that he was an ET, pointing out that he was extra to the terrestrial realm.

In further direct conversations with upstairs we have been told not to compartmentalise. It was suggested that we acknowledge that the demarcation lines between the areas of spirit and the off world energies, so to speak, are becoming more and more blurred. Where does the one end and the other begin?

Chapter 12

Earth Healing

We now come to the main thrust or reason for all that you have been concerned with as you have Worked your way through these pages, Healing the Planet Beneath Your Feet. As The Merlin summarised it, we are Working towards making good the damage that mankind has inflicted upon a defenceless, long suffering Earth.

Over the total surface of the Earth there are myriad lines of energies of varying frequencies. In order to best understand them look on them as the veins and arteries of the body on the surface of the skin. Each and everyone of them is essential in the continuing existence of the planet. Many people make the claim that there are positive and negative energies, consistent with the ideas of good and evil. I categorically deny this way of thinking. Yes there are positive and negative energies, as in active and passive.

I have heard it claimed that whole streets are under the influence of bad energies. These energies causing people to become ill and die. I get quite angry when I hear these sort of things said or written. The lines of energy were there before we came along and built our house. Our ancestors knew of them and made due allowances for the effects of these lines. Building either away from them or in alignment with them.

From personal experience we have discovered that if we want to get a really good night's sleep then, whilst at home and in the United States of America, we should sleep with our heads to the South and our feet to the North, in line with the current flow about us. However in Iceland we need our heads to the East and our feet to the West. There are some very different currents in those snowy wastes.

Checking up on the 'bad streets' we have ascertained that the all the houses are out of line with the energy lines. It is this that creates the sense of being unwell, not the line itself. Blame whoever you like, but not the Earth. It was there first. As a further example of our disregard for the Earth Energy Lines (sometimes referred to as Ley Lines) let me tell you of something we came across not too far from our home in Norfolk.

Just outside the Trowse Newton suburb of Norwich there is an old wood henge which has been carefully allowed to remain. The farmer who owns the field in which it lies is forbidden to plough it. Henges, like the famous Stonehenge which is Northwest of Salisbury in Wiltshire, mark cross-over points where two or more lines intersect. Having been prompted by our mentors to get over and have a look, we were horrified to find that to the Northeast of the henge there is an electricity sub-station and two lines of pylons marched across the field and went right over the top of this little henge. June and I shifted our perceptions and were even more horrified to discover that there were absolutely no Earth Energy Lines at the henge surface. Where were they? You can't just rub them out.

Advancing into the centre of the henge we extended our awareness and found them. At a guess we considered the Lines to be some five miles below the surface. Some aspect of the electro-magnetic energy radiating from the high voltage cables strung overhead had pushed the Lines down below the surface. We knew that we had to get them back on the surface and after a lot of thought and confirmation from The Merlin we got stuck into it.

What we did was construct a thought-form reflective dome over the entire henge, leaving a ground level gap of one or two feet all around the base. We worked on this for a complete Moon Phase of twenty-eight days. On the night preceding the Summer Solstice of 1992, a group of us gathered at 2 a.m. and found that the dome had already started the Work for us. The Lines had risen of their own accord to some two miles below the surface. All we were required to do was to lift them the last part and with the two Swords stapled the four Energy Lines back onto the surface. The dome is still in place and the Lines are holding firm. The Earth is doing its thing as it should in that area.

2 a.m.? Most of our Earth Healing Work is done in the dead of night. Quantum physics is teaching us that Light is energy and can interfere with other energies, therefore to Work in the dark cuts down any such intrusions. If you go into hospital for an operation, what do they do to you before the scalpels come out? They put you to sleep. So it is with the Earth. When the Sun is on the opposite side of the planet, the part that we are standing upon is ostensibly asleep. We can operate without undue trauma to the patient. The Earth awakes (just as you, the surgical patient, would awaken) with the job done and is able to recuperate of its own accord. There is also the factor of other aware people in the vicinity who are not involved in the process. If they had any sense they will be at home in bed and sound asleep, oblivious to what we're doing. If there were to be any 'tremor in the force' as the operation was being carried out, they would not be aware of it and be unsettled by it. Awaking the following morning our aware person may just feel a little out of sorts and put it down to another restless night and shrug it off and get on with Life. It is a part of the way we Work that we come and go, doing our Work, without anyone knowing where, when or why. No markers are ever left. We are all both nameless and faceless.

As we had first flown across the Atlantic I had wondered why we were being sent to Pittsburgh, Pennsylvania, of all places. We hadn't been there too long before we discovered the reason. Doing the tourist bit, our hostess had taken us to the Pittsburgh Point, where the Allegheny and Monongahela Rivers join to form the Ohio River. Standing on the point I shifted my perception and looked at the natural vortex of energy that is at the confluence of any river. In my view it was reeling drunkenly on its base tip. It was pretty close to falling over. As I questioned the reason for this I had been informed that the area all about Pittsburgh had been heavily mined, not just underground but also with the open cast strip mines, plus there were any number of tunnels torn through the surrounding hills. All this had destabilised the vortex.

I faced a dilemma. At that time the Twin Rivers Arts Festival was in full swing with obviously some late night revelry. How did I, we, get to the Point at 2 a.m. carrying the two Swords? The Dragon Sword is 47 inches long and not just tucked in a pocket. How would the local constabulary react? I became extremely nervous. My advisors came to my rescue as we had stood on the Washington Heights overlooking the Point. They advised me to set the two Swords up in our room, which was only a mile or so away from the Point, and bend a beam of energy from them over the city and down through the centre of the vortex, like sugar candy (candy-floss) on a stick. Back in the house I had done as requested and sent the beam. For three days it had run. At the end of which I was advised to turn it off. The information came that this energy had gone down the centre of the vortex and then radiated outwards for a distance of 100 miles and restabilised all the energies within that area. Task completed.

In a slightly different manner, I have mentioned, in passing, the Working at Thingvellir in Iceland. The locals had advised us that there was a general sense of unease at this historic spot and they had wondered what we would make of it. When Lief Erikson had first landed in 954 AD the settlers had chosen the beautiful, natural site at Thingvellir as the centre of their governmental formation. Here they had met and sorted out their legalities for the colony. Iceland did not escape the Inquisition. Supposed Witches were taken to Thingvellir and thrown into a watery maelstrom. If they sank and were drowned they were deemed innocent. If they floated and survived they were guilty and were dragged out and killed. Some no win situation? As we had fought our way through crotch deep snow to the bridge over the raging waters I had put out a call to the Guardian of Place and advised of our presence. The Guardian had immediately appeared in my altered perception. It had appeared as a very large vortex of energy, but beside it, tiny in the corner of my vision, were two small vortices. I had zeroed in on these two and found that they were what I perceived to be the energies of two of the unfortunate ladies who had been drowned. I spent some time in telepathic conversation with these two ladies and finally convinced them that they needn't hang around the pool any longer and invited them to move on. They conceded and disappeared from my vision.

Another job done. Much later I was given a very severe slapped wrist. I was told, in no uncertain terms, that there are no such things as 'lost spirits'. Everyone goes home! Everyone is met and escorted wherever they wish to go. The two vortices were, in fact, 'thought-forms' created by the many visitors. Somehow or other I had used my Magical Mental Energy to disperse them.

As you can see, there are many ways of Working with the Earth Energies, but it all relies upon an acceptance of the responsibilities inherent in being an Earth Healer. Without putting too fine a point on it, these pages are about magic, mental magic. We are constantly being advised on the power of the mind and that thoughts are energy. I have found this to be so in the realms of Earth Healing.

There are many kinds of magic. Ceremonial, High, Low, White, Black, etc.. Religious and atheistic magicians, but, in my experience, most of us are agnostic. Constantly questioning everything we come across in our individual quests. Whatever magic we Work it rests in the power of the mind. For instance, in Ceremonial Magic the magician stands in the physical temple and physically holds a sword aloft, but in their mind they are standing in another 'temple not built by hands' holding aloft the sword of another realm. That is where the magic is. In the other realm. The physical object here is merely an instrument upon which the magician can fix the mind to transfer the thought elsewhere.

Perhaps you're not aware of being in a temple not built by hands, such as the Dragon Stones for instance, but assume that you are and it will follow that you will be, and in the fullness of time you will find that your sensitivity will become finely attuned and you will begin to sense where you are and where you are facing. Trust is the keyword. Trust yourself, your abilities and the spirit within. Always Work on the 'as if' principle.

Let us get down to the serious business of Earth Healing and open with a simple scenario. You are sitting in your home relaxing after a busy day. You are quietly contemplating those activities when suddenly you hear the sound of voices under your windows. Rising, you look out and see people clambering over your property bringing pots of paint to decorate the outside of your home. As if that wasn't bad enough, their idea of a colour scheme makes your stomach heave. You verbally chastise them for disturbing you. Their response is that they were passing and saw that the property was in need of restoration so had decided to lend a hand. You point out that if they had knocked at the door and discussed the problem then perhaps some sort of mutual agreement could have been reached whereby your property could be restored, but in a manner that you, as the owner, would be comfortable with.

The Merlin went to great lengths to make me not only see, but understand, that in effect Planet Earth belongs to the Elemental Kingdoms and the World of Faerie. The Elementals are fairly well known as Earth, Air, Fire and Water, but the World of Faerie is still only little known. As I understand it, the World of Faerie is the energy that operates under the influence of the Elementals and actually causes all plants to grow. A nature life force impetus.

For the moment, that is all that you need to know at this time. Why? Because the initial aim of the following Visualisation Exercises is not only to introduce yourself to the Owners of Planet Earth, but also for you to gain an understanding of them. With the harmony of the common knowledge in the rapport between them and you, there will be ways that you as a unique individual can assist in the overall Work. They will understand far better than you what exactly you can do. They will note and use your strong, positive points and, as a bonus, help you to turn your negative attributes to positive ends. For instance. As a much younger person I was often getting into trouble for talking too much. I now spend my time teaching, lecturing and doing tarot readings. The negative of too much talk is now a positive attribute, thanks to the other realms advice and guidance.

However many people have come to me in the past claiming that they have no visualisational ability and bemoaning their lack of apparent clairvoyant ability. I'll let you into a little secret. The vast majority of those who claim to be clairvoyant aren't. They are clairsentient. Clairvoyance is the ability to see non-corporate entities. Clairsentience, on the other hand, is clear sensing. Few really do see. Most sense the presence of the spiritual or other energy. This sensing allows the person to feel whether the contacted spirit is male or female, young or old, tall or short, slim or fat, bearded, bald, or whatever. Another secret is about to be let out of the bag.

When we are Working we are normally concentrating extremely hard and are far too busy to be really aware of what is going on around us, but we act on the 'as if' principle. To get back to our little analogy. Earlier we spoke of the magician raising a physical sword. They are concentrating on the effect this action will have in the other realm so that they can bend that energy to its Work. In many instances the magician will neither see nor be aware of the actual raising of the non-physical sword, but Works on the assumption that the sword is rising and that the energy so produced is combining in readiness for the outcome. The magician is Working on the 'as if' principle.

Okay, lets get started. Where, when and how do we get involved with all of this? Straight off, there is a gentle Exercise that you can do whenever you wish. The other realms have agreed to accept this from those they do not yet know. They assure me that it makes a very real contribution to the overall effort. It is so simple that anyone can do it, even if they decide not to go any further than simply reading these pages. The Planet needs all the help it can get. Just read it through a couple of times to get the idea in your mind, then spend a few seconds whenever you have the time doing it.

Imagine you are standing in your favourite outdoor, natural, location. Mountains, trees, lakes, meadows, plains, deserts, rivers, wherever. It may be day or night; dawn or dusk; whichever you find the most comfortable.

Be aware of a Beam of Pure, Brilliant Energy descending from the unknown depths of space and coming down beside you, around you or through you. With enhanced vision you are able to watch the Beam of Energy enter the surface of the Planet and travel through to the very centre of the core of the Planet.

When it reaches that central point it radiates in all directions and passes outward through the Planet's body and back into space, where it arcs back towards the unknown source from which it came, creating a completed circuit.

The Earth Healing Invocation is simple.

"May the Energy of Healing pass to the core of this our Planet and, as it returns, bring Healing to all that is in the Earth, all that is on the Earth, and all that is about the Earth. Returning to its source so that the circuit is complete."

That's a little taster, now lets get down to the nitty gritty by looking at how to achieve the maximum results from minimum effort. However it must be stressed that the Exercises not only serve as a plus factor for the Planet, but will also have a marked effect on the lives of those who undertake such activities. I make no apologies for the fact that you will find that there will be repercussions in your lives. You are opening yourselves to Forces and Powers which are undreamed of in the normal daily round of the physical, workaday world.

The corner stone of these Exercises is Personal Responsibility. Accepting the processes and ramifications that will change not only the environment, but yourself as well, in ways that no one can foresee. What will happen to you will be unique in the total experience of the world and how you deal with it is entirely down to you, no one else. Each Exercise is a further step along a Path of Progression and should not be undertaken lightly. They are not toys nor games to be used as play things. They are for real and must be treated with respect.

Stick with the simplicity of the Exercises as laid down, even if there is the temptation to modify little bits here and there. Don't. The Merlin advised me that we have to learn to conform before we can be a non-conformist. Once you have mastered all of the Exercises, then you can adapt things however you wish. By then you will have sufficient experience to allow such freedom of action.

I acknowledge that the layout of the energies may not be exactly as you know them to be, but we are in times of change. There are many ideas and concepts being developed. Many are good, but some are merely fad, fancy or fashion and will pass away as if they have never been. What is shown here is centuries old, tried, tested and found true for us. These Exercises are based on the image of the Pre-Christian Stone Circles of Ancient Britain. Perhaps wherever you are a particular Elemental may normally be at a different Compass Point. In talking with the Elementals in other Lands around the World they accept the notions shown here and will gladly be flexible in their approach to your completion of these Exercises.

There are a number of Exercises and should be dealt with one at a time, not moving from the First to the Second, for instance, until you have complete mastery of the First. Complete the current Exercise every day for five consecutive days, than take two days off. You need a regular break to assimilate the knock-on effects of being in contact with those you are about to meet. Five minutes a day for five days will bring far superior results in comparison to twenty-five minutes once a week.

Those of you that are already aware, and Working, may well find that visions will arise as normal, however, these must be Rejected Totally. They are not what these Exercise are about. Here we are dealing with Control. Your control of your mind. A spontaneous vision is uncontrolled and uncontrollable. Get rid of it. Some of you that have been Working under another regime may find that those might cease whilst you are Working with these. Don't be alarmed, it is a natural part of the Work, and if it has stopped there is a very strong possibility that it will return in the fullness of time.

To add a little flavour we all create another identity for ourselves when we go visiting. A sort of magical persona. It may sound extremely romantic and flamboyant, but it helps in recognising that we are no longer Joe Bloggs, candle-stick maker, or Jane Smith, domestic environmental engineer (housewife). In the magical worlds we can be whatever we would wish to be. Magus or Warrior Queen. Your choice. As I said it is a bit fanciful, but the Work that you will carry out will compensate for your little foibles.

Create an identity for yourself. We tend to start by creating a mental image of a physical body to inhabit. This is often referred to as your Body of Light. If, like me, you are overweight, balding, unfit, short of stature, etc., then visualise yourself as you would truly wish to be. Tall, lithe, slim and athletic? Dark hair, light hair? Whatever you desire. Visualise how you would truly like to be. On the wrong side of fifty? Want to be in your prime? Twenty five, thirty? Then recreate how you were, but amend it with the previous paragraph. Be as you would wish to be. It is the only real choice that you will have in this Work.

Myth, legend and tradition tells us that to know the name of someone gives one an element of control over that person. Whether this is strictly true or not is debatable, however for the time being act as if it is so. There is a lot of thought required in determining exactly what you wish to be known as on the other levels. This name should be a marked indication of your aspirations in regard to the Work and equally how you intend to carry it through . As mentioned earlier Mrs Violet Mary Firth for instance was a highly respected magician, but not under that name. Her magical name almost became common knowledge as she wrote extensively. The name properly was Deo Non Fortuna meaning God, not Fate. She is well known now as Dion Fortune.

Having given things a lot of serious thought and decided what you intend to call yourself, there is then the requirement to make your name and you known to the other realms. A sort of baptism, to use a term, makes this an easy exercise, notwithstanding that it will have serious overtones in the longer term future.

The Merlin suggested the following as an outline idea. With this, and all the following Exercises, read it through a few times until you have it firmly in your mind before you begin. Or you can, if you wish, read it onto a tape and then get comfortable and play it back to yourself whilst visualising what is going on. Why don't you give it a whirl?

You are in your room in your Body of Light.

A ball of brilliant colourless Energy appears about six feet in front of you, slightly above your head height.

You acknowledge its presence, whereupon in response a gentle beam of light comes from the Ball and expanding bathes you in its light.

You call, softly but penetratingly along the beam of light the name you wish to be known by.

As the name is accepted so a short needle-like ray of golden light is emitted from the Ball and impinges on your forehead in a gesture of acceptance.

The Ball withdraws the beam of light, disappears and you disperse your Body of Light, returning to the physical world.

Do not feel that once you have named yourself you are stuck with it. As you evolve, so should your aspirations as well. Having formally introduced yourself in your first name, it is relatively easy to change it at a later date. Approach whichever aspect you are then Working with in your first identity and, politely, request that you be known by your newly chosen name from that time onwards. Its that easy.

However, they may also decide that you need a new name. They will give it to you. Listen, make sure you've got it right, then, when you come back, have a serious think over the connotations of what they have called you. Don't, whatever you do, get carried away with lots of fanciful notions over some of the grandiouse names they might stick you with. These names are not for this world, and pale into almost insignificance when placed in context in regard to the Cosmos and beyond.

Let's get down to some serious business and prepare ourselves for the future Work.

Exercise 1: The Dragon Stones

The aims of this simple Exercise operate on many levels. Firstly, we need a safe, secure, sacred place where we will be reasonably comfortable. Secondly, we are aiming for Earth Healing, therefore we need to be in the right sort of environment for such endeavours. Thirdly, it should not be over elaborate. You will need to build it in your mind time and time again until it becomes an automatic reflex and exists for you as more than a mind construction.

I well remember joining a group of people who had come together to reconstruct Solomon's Temple for future Work. We were Working on it off and on all day, it took nine hours. You and I don't have the time to waste so much energy for such things. We need something simple, yet striking.

Get yourself comfortable, and secure in your physical area. Pay due regard to the 'rules' mentioned before. Relax and follow through the following :

It is that moment of the night that immediately precedes the dawn. The moon has set and above your head the stars glisten in the dark heavens.

You are aware that you stand on a plain of broad rolling grassy hills.

A chill breeze blows gently yet persistently against your face and your clothing rustles against your body.

As your eyes adjust to the encircling gloom you become aware of a horse-shoe of six Megalithic Stones in front of and about you. The centre pair immediately in front of you have a cap-stone bridging them forming a trilithon.

Between you and the trilithon lies another stone, on its side in the grass much like an altar.

Behind you, closing the mouth of the horse-shoe, is a pool of water.

There is an air of expectancy, a sense of stillness and waiting.

Dimly, through the trilithon, you become aware of a strip of cold light edging the distant horizon. Slowly it expands across the whole of the Eastern edge of the landscape.

In the grass about the Stones you begin to hear the rustle of small creatures and insects as they stir from their slumbers and begin the quest for food and sustenance.

Still the dawn light grows and the breeze blows chill against you.

Within the trilithon a sliver of the sun peeps over the edge of the world and a brilliant golden ray of light flashes across the land, through the stones, and surrounds you. Strong as this ray is, it neither blinds nor hurts the eyes.

You raise your arms until you stand as a letter 'Y' in salutation to the Light and warmth that rides that ray. With the coming of that ray, the breeze disappears, and the warmth spreads deeply through your body, driving the chill from within and setting your blood racing in the heat.

As the sun slowly rises, so the ray of light expands as it courses across the land, through the trilithon, about you and through you.

The sun finally clears the horizon and for a brief moment the trilithon becomes a portal of total Light, blazing with golden brilliance.

The moment is too short for as suddenly as it came the ray disappears and you lower your arms.

There may be a sense of regret, however there is a sure and certain knowledge that you have the right to return and participate in this event whenever you wish.

Your gaze wanders idly about the scene and you drink in the solitary splendour of these age old Stones, and hear the call of birds heralding the new day. All is at peace, ready to face whatever may come your way.

Return to yourself and re-awaken your body by flexing your muscles.

Before proceeding with your life, it is important to make a journal or diary entry of your feelings, etc., that were experienced during the exercise. It should be made immediately you have finished, whilst things are still fresh in your mind.

Be honest with yourself. It is for your eyes only. Nobody else need ever read them. It is equally important to write a 'Nil Report', or 'Nothing Felt', etc.. These reports are just as much a part of your progression as the time that you finally make the stars and beyond. Do not be put off by long periods of nothing; it happens sometimes. Having written your report, have a cup of coffee, tea or milk and a biscuit. Having a snack and a drink helps you to return to the physical.

Once you have fully mastered this Exercise, and not before, you should be ready to move on to communicating with the Elementals. I am going to offer two different ways to communicate with them. Firstly by way of investing them with human forms and secondly by Working with the Vortices of Energy. Both are equally viable and you will arrive at the same result either way. It is your choice. Use whichever you initially feel comfortable with.

We start with the human forms. Those that you are being introduced to will be described as tradition demands in a masculine form, however, they are neither male nor female, but androgynous. It has to be emphasised that there is no such thing as gender, in the way that we know it, in these other realms. We refer to them as Kings, giving them their ancient well known names for convenience sake, simply as they are deemed to rule a Kingdom.

At certain points in these exercises you are requested to pay your respects. Do whatever you feel is correct. Some visualise themselves going down on one knee, bowing the head. Others simply nod. To reiterate, do whatever you feel the occasion warrants, but remember, courtesy costs nothing and achieves everything.

In this, and subsequent Exercises there is an important Realisation that must be fully appreciated before proceeding to the next Exercise. In order to remove any confusion it is important that you fully understand what is meant by a Realisation. It is natural to understand a thing intellectually. It is equally natural to understand something emotionally. The tricky part is understanding through both. Bluntly, it is almost a gut reaction. The understanding strikes both the heart and the mind in a moment of illumination.

Exercise 2: Elemental Air

The aim of this Exercise is to meet, and gain acceptance from, Elemental Air.

(Complete Exercise 1 up to the point where the sun has risen and you have lowered your arms.)

You pause for a moment, gazing into the Eastern trilithon and directing thereto your wish for an audience with the King of the Air

You start forward, passing to the North of the 'altar' stone and move to the centre of the trilithon where you pause. During this moment you announce yourself and request permission to pass through.

Permission is granted and you step forward confidently.

As you exit the far side of the trilithon the scene of the rolling hills disappears and you find yourself at the beginning of a tunnel of light grey luminescence.

The walls and floor seem to flow with movement. This is merely an illusion and beneath your questing feet you feel the solidity of a sure path. The tunnel rises very gently and you ascend without effort.

It is a short tunnel and soon opens into the form of a large cavern in the sky. The floor appears to be of clouds, which rise up the walls. The roof is the colour of the most beautiful azure blue of high summer. There is an airy, spacious, feeling to the whole of the cavern.

Down either side of the cavern, but leaving a clear straight path for you, stand ethereal figures of every shade of yellow and gold. The sylphs, the people of the Kingdom of the Air.

You move confidently forward towards a high throne on a low dais at the far end of the cavern.

Some of the sylphs eye you warily, others ignore you. There is slight sense of tension from them. A waiting.

Having passed along the pathway you come to the clearing before the dais and stop, paying your respects to the throne stating your name.

Your eyes focus on the throne, which appears to be made of a single solid cloud and the figure seated thereon. It is a man, clothed in the various shades of yellow and gold upon his robes, but the shadings blend subtly into one another. On his head there is a cap, vaguely reminiscent of a bird's head, with the bill upon his forehead stopping short of his eyebrows. Atop this cap is a crown apparently made of cloud but solid and real, glistening in the sky light. From his shoulders and arms depends a cape, symbolising the wings of a bird. Light tawny eyes regard you steadily from either side of a hawk nose over tight thin lips.

His Majesty Paraldar, King of the Air and Ruler of the Skies, acknowledges your respects with a nod of the head and the slight wave of a hand.

The realisation comes that here is the Seat of Wisdom in the World. True Wisdom, not that which passes for such in the World of Man.

He recognises your adjustment and the face relaxes into a slight smile.

"Welcome to the Kingdom of the Air. What do you seek?" his voice whispers across the space between you.

You give thanks for his welcome and politely state your reason for seeking this audience.

He responds suitably and rises to his feet. The audience is over. You pay your respects and he departs, leaving you to return to the Dragon Stones.

You turn to walk back along the path and the sylphs acknowledge your departure. Their King has accepted you therefore so do they.

It is but a short journey back down the tunnel and you stand within the trilithon in the sunlight.

Passing to the South of the altar you return to your original position and pause.

Return to yourself and re-awaken your muscles.

Write up your report immediately, including exactly what your request was and exactly what his Majesty's response was, plus your understanding of the realisation.

A drink and a snack to bring you back to normal.

Exercise 3: Elemental Fire
The aim of this Exercise is to meet, and gain acceptance from, Elemental Fire.

(Complete Exercise 1 up to the point where the sun has risen and you have lowered your arms.)

You pause for a moment, turn to your right and look towards the two Southern Stones gazing through the gap between them, directing your wish thereto for an audience with the King of Fire.

You move to the centre of the two stones where you pause again. You mentally announce your name and request permission to pass through.

Permission is granted and you step forward confidently. Exiting the stones you find a tunnel of flame and fire. Apparently it is all ablaze, but there is neither heat nor burning to bother you. It is another illusion. Once again your questing feet find firm footings and you step forward in confidence along the short level tunnel into the cavern of fire.

In size and shape it is very similar to the cave of the Air, but the floor and walls are the colours of liquid fire, whilst the ceiling is a very light bright grey rolling billow of smoke.

The ethereal figures in attendance are every shade of red and orange. The salamanders, the people of fire.

Once again as you proceed down the central path the salamanders take little or no notice of you. Where you are seen there is wariness.

You stop in the clearing before the throne and pay your respects, stating your name.

Your eyes focus on the throne which appears to be made of a single solid flame, and the figure seated thereon. It is a man, clothed in the various shades of red and orange robes, but the shadings blend subtly into one another. Atop his head is a crown, apparently of flame, but solid and real flashing in the firelight. Light pink eyes regard you steadily from either side of a slender nose over tight thin lips.

His Majesty, Djinn, King of Fire and Ruler of the Flames, acknowledges your respects with a nod of the head and the slight wave of a hand.

The realisation comes that here is the Seat of Energy in the World. He recognises your adjustment and his face relaxes into a slight smile.

"Welcome to the Kingdom of Fire. What do you seek?" his voice crackles to you.

You thank him for his welcome and state your reasons for attending.

He responds suitably and rises to his feet. The audience is over. You pay your respects as he departs, leaving you to return to the Stones.

You turn to leave down the central path and the salamanders acknowledge your departure. Their King has accepted you, therefore so do they.

Back along the tunnel to stand between the Southern stones in the sunlight.

You move back to your original position and pause before returning to yourself.

Write up you report immediately, noting exactly what your request was, his response and your understanding of the realisation received. A drink and a snack.

Exercise 4: Elemental Water

The aim of this Exercise is to meet, and gain acceptance from, Elemental Water.

(Complete Exercise 1 up to the point where the sun has risen and you have lowered your arms.)

You pause for a moment, turning to your right you turn about and look towards the pool of water, directing your wish thereto for an audience with the King of Water.

You move to the waters edge and pause to announce your name and request permission to enter.

Permission is granted and you step confidently into the tunnel that has opened in the waters, leading gently down into the depths. Once again your questing feet find firm footings as you walk to the cavern of Water.

In size and shape this is very similar to the other caverns. The floor is the colour of the deep dark blue of the ocean and the walls are a lighter blue. The ceiling is a very light bright blue/grey with shifting sparkles of light, as of sunlight on the surface.

The ethereal figures in attendance are every shade of blue. The undines, the people of water.

Once again as you proceed down the central path, the undines take little or no notice of you. Where you are seen, there is wariness.

You stop in the clearing before the throne, paying your respects and stating your name.

You focus on the throne, which appears to be made of a single billowing wave, and the figure seated thereon. It is a man, clothed in various shades of blue, the shadings blending subtly. Atop his head is a crown, apparently made of spume, but solid, flashing in the reflected light. Light piercing blue eyes regard you steadily from either side of an aquiline nose over tight thin lips.

His Majesty, Neksa, King of Water and Ruler of the Waves, acknowledges your respects with a nod of the head and the slight wave of a hand.

The realisation comes that here is the Seat of Power in the world. True power, not that which passes for such in the world of man.

He recognises your adjustment and the face relaxes into a slight smile.

"Welcome to the Kingdom of Water. What do you seek?" bubbles his voice.

You thank him and state your reasons for attending.

He responds suitably and rises to his feet. The audience is over and you pay your respects as he leaves. You turn back down the pathway and the undines acknowledge your departure. Their King has accepted you therefore so do they.

Through the tunnel and you stand on the waters edge in the sunlight.

Move back to the centre of the Dragon Stones, pause, and then return to yourself.

Write up you report immediately, noting exactly what your request was, his response and your understanding of the realisation received. A drink and a snack.

Exercise 5: Elemental Earth

The aim of this Exercise is to meet, and gain acceptance from, Elemental Earth.

(Complete Exercise 1 up to the point where the sun has risen and you have lowered your arms.)

You pause for a moment, turning to your right you face towards the Northern stones, directing your wish thereto for an audience with the King of Earth.

You move to those stones, pause, announce your name and request permission to enter.

Permission is granted and you step confidently forward between the two stones into a tunnel that has opened in the ground leading gently down. Firm footing leads you to the cavern of the Earth.

This cavern is similar in size and shape to the others. The floor, walls and ceiling are all the colours of granite, marble, coal, gold, silver and other minerals which sparkle with an inner light, illuminating the cavern.

The ethereal figures are every shade of black, brown and the darker greens. The gnomes, the people of the Earth, who take little or no notice of you as you move down the pathway. Where you are seen there is wariness.

You stop before the throne, pay your respects and state your name.

You focus on the throne which appears to be made of a single multi-coloured rock, and the figure seated thereon. It is a man, clothed in the various shades of black, brown and the darker greens, subtly blending. Atop his head is a crystal crown which flashes with an inner light of its own. Dark, piercing black eyes regard your steadily from either side of a roman nose over tight thin lips.

His Majesty, Ghobb, King of Earth and Ruler of the Land, acknowledges your respects with the slightest nod of the head.

The realisation comes the here is the seat of the Transmutation and Mediation of all the Wisdom, Energy and Power directed hereto from the other Kingdoms.

He recognises your adjustment and he relaxes.

"Welcome to the Kingdom of the Earth. What do you seek?" he grates.

You give thanks and state your reasons for attending.

He responds suitably and rises. The audience is over and you pay your respects as he departs.

You turn and leave down the pathway. The gnomes acknowledge you. Their King has accepted you, therefore so do they.

Back in the Dragon Stones you move back to the centre, pause, and then return to yourself.

Write up you report immediately, noting exactly what your request was, his response and your understanding of the realisation received. A drink and a snack.

Having completed these Exercises fully you should now be in a position to Work with the Elementals. The Kings, or a representative, will visit with you in the Dragon Stones and they will guide you into the Work that you can do with them.

You now have an alliance and you will find that they will utilise your personal, unique abilities to the furtherance of the Work. Well done.

However, even if you haven't, as yet, fully completed these Exercises you can still participate in the Seasonal Changes at the Equinoxes and Solstices, which are important to the Elemental Kingdoms.

Chapter 13

Seasonal Rites

In Working Rites the 'rules', such as they are, remain the same. Be comfortable, have dedication and commitment, lay your plans in regard to normal daily life, keep your diary up to date. Just because you are Working doesn't mean that there won't be any personal information for you.

As I said, it is not necessary for you to have completed, nor even started, meeting the Kings. However, you do need a Working knowledge of the Dragon Stones. If it is at all possible, try and carry through the Workings in a natural environment. In woods, beside a lake, on the seashore, in the mountains. It adds a tremendous depth of feeling, which is enhanced by the fact that you have made a special effort to be where you are.

Whilst I have to introduce a number of other energies at this point I have found that some information is best based upon personal discovery so have kept the introduction to a minimum. Don't be concerned at this lack of information as all of these energies are on your side and will not harm you in any way. To repeat, the only danger to you is created by you. Not them.

The Guardian of Place. This is the combined energy of any place. It is the vibration of the woods, the forest, the valley, wherever. It is a sort of ambassador for all the Kingdoms. Wherever you go to Work always ask permission of the place before you start. I have always found it preferable to ask at least a day before Working, but I acknowledge that this may not always be practical.

I have mentioned the World of Faerie before, but now we are going to making contact with them. You'll recall that I said that they are a form of the life force impetus. I have called the sovereigns King Oberon and Queen Titania, but they are merely names of convenience; easily remembered.

Next there is the energy of the Guardian of Nature. I have called this Pan, because, once again, it is an easy name to remember and fairly well known; even if for the wrong reasons.

We now move into the tricky bits. Earlier you would have read that I had been Working with an energy called The Merlin. In our circle he stands in the East. It is not a man, but it is a masculine energy. He is a British energy which operates within mainland Britain. Having said this, however, each continent has a masculine energy of its own as well. The problem is in identifying it. This is because it is of a far more subtle vibration than the Elemental Kingdoms. As a result of my travels I have been able to meet and commune with two other masculine energies. The first is a part of the Americas, North and South. For ease of reference I have referred to it simply as the Grandfather. In Iceland it is a Giant Man, whose name is both unpronounceable and unprintable. For the benefit of these pages I'll just refer to this particular energy as the Masculine; you might wish to investigate your Land's Masculine Energy and its identity more fully at a later date.

The feminine aspect, which stands in the West of our circle, in Britain I have called The Lady of the Lake. In the Americas I have spoken with her in the guise of the Grandmother. In Iceland she is a Bull - I don't fully understand it either, yet. For these pages I'll refer to this simply as the Feminine.

In the South of the circle we have what we refer to as the Dragon Energies. These are most easily understood as the combined energies of all the Ley Lines and such. Its more than that, but that will do for now. Once again, each Land has its own unique Dragon. For ease of reference, this will be termed as the Dragon.

149

In the North there is what I call the Senior Guardian of the Land. Here in Britain I refer to it as Herne the Hunter. In the Americas I have taken the Hopi name of Masàw for this energy. In Iceland, it takes the form of an Eagle. Once again, unpronounceable. For these pages it will just be the Senior Guardian.

All of these energies are geographical. To a degree, for instance, it is possible to Work with Masàw in Britain, but not nearly with the Power and Force of Working with it in the Americas. Personal experience has proved it beyond any doubt in my mind.

Enjoy the rite. Live it but do not make a spectacle of yourself. This is about Working, not making a side-show.

It is stressed that in these and any other rites you must only visualise yourself. No other person alive or dead should figure in your Working. It could lead to problems, not only for you, but for the person visualised as well. The fact that a group of you have gathered together to celebrate the rite is immaterial. Each of you stands alone.

It is suggested that you read through the complete rite a few times to get the flavour of what is going on. There is no slavish dogma here. The idea behind the rite is the important thing, so do not feel bound to follow them to the letter. Adapt the central theme to your own unique individual personality. Be yourself.

Winter Solstice
(Approximately December 19 or 20.)

It is night and you stand, alone, in the centre of the Dragon Stones facing the Eastern trilithon. The moon has set and you can see the stars with the utmost clarity in the cloudless sky. There is only starlight.

After a while you begin to feel yourself lighten and find that you are gently rising into the air, with the Dragon Stones dropping away below you.

You pass out through the atmosphere into space. You see the sun and find that you are moving towards it, gathering speed as you go.

You become aware of the solar winds and that the depths of space are not empty, there are currents, motion, movement and life. Life after another order, after another manner, but life nonetheless.

As you are nearing the sun you realise that the brightness of it does not cause any discomfort to your eyes.

When the sun totally fills your vision you come to a halt.

You raise your arms into the 'Y' of salutation and give thanks for the light that has fallen on the Earth throughout the year, aiding the plants to grow and ripen for the harvest.

As you commune with the sun you acknowledge its symbolism as the sustainer of all life. It is a source through which the power of life comes to all.

You lower your arms and turn to begin the journey back to the Earth. Once again you are aware of the currents that flow through space.

You become aware that you are slowing to a halt in the darkness just short of the planet.

You find that you are close to the moon and you turn to face it. In the 'Y' salute you acknowledge the moon as a part of the life force of the planet. The reflector of the sun's light during the night and the instigator of the tides; not just of the seas, but of all life. Acknowledge that the moon is an integral part of the sustainer of life.

Lower your arms and head for the Earth again.

Moving back into the atmosphere you see that you are returning to the Dragon Stones. Very gently you land in the centre facing the trilithon.

You walk forward, passing to the North of the altar, to the trilithon. You stand within the trilithon not passing through.

You call for Paraldar, King of the Air. The scene before you wavers. You state your name. He stands before you with the sylphs behind him.

You pay your respects and state that you have come to say thank you for the air that has moved this year and to advise that it is the time of the Winter Solstice and that the Kingdom should be at peace to rest and sleep until the Spring, when you will return to awaken them.

You repeat your respects and the scene disappears.

You turn to your right and walk around the Southern edge of the altar to the Southern stones, where you stand between them.

You call for Djinn, King of Fire. The scene before you wavers. You state your name. He stands before you with the salamanders behind him.

You pay your respects and state that you have come to say thank you for the fires that have warmed the Earth and to advise that it is the time of the Winter Solstice and that the Kingdom should be at peace to rest and sleep until the Spring, when you will return to awaken them.

You repeat your respects and the scene disappears.

You step back and turn to your right to walk to the waters edge of the Western pool of water where you call for Neksa, King of the Waters. The scene before you wavers. You state your name. He stands before you with the undines behind him.

You pay your respects and state that you have come to say thank you for the waters of life that have moved this year and to advise that it is the time of the Winter Solstice and that it is time for the Earth to recuperate in readiness for the new crops next year. You ask that the rains should be allowed to fall and that the Kingdom should be at peace to rest and sleep until the Spring, when you will return to awaken them.

You repeat your respects and the scene disappears.

You turn to your right and walk to stand between the Northern stones.

You call for Ghobb, King of Earth. The scene before you wavers. You state your name. He stands before you with the gnomes behind him.

You pay your respects and state that you have come to say thank you to the Earth. You give notice that it is the time of the Winter Solstice. You also state that you have met his brothers and asked for their aid in the restoration of the earth and that the Kingdom of the Earth should now be at peace to rest and sleep until the Spring, when you will return to awaken them.

You repeat your respects and the scene disappears.

You turn to your right and move to the centre side of the altar stone, where you look down upon the top.

You call for King Oberon and Queen Titania, Sovereigns of the World of Faerie. A small mist swirls on the top of the stone. You state your name. The two of them stand in miniature before you.

You pay your respects and state that you have come to say thank you for the tireless, ceaseless Work of this year and to advise that it is the time of the Winter Solstice and that the Kingdom should be at peace to rest and sleep until the Spring, when you will return to awaken them.

You repeat your respects and the scene disappears.

You back to the centre and stand quietly; waiting.

You become aware of a Dome of Force pulsing over the whole of the Dragon Stones. A quivering of the atmosphere. It is Pan, the Guardian of Nature.

You pay your respects and state your name.

You advise that you have come to say thank you for the year that has come to an end and also that you have spoken with Elemental Kingdoms and requested that the Earth should sleep for the winter. You finally advise that you have undertaken to return at the change of season to re-awaken them.

You repeat your respects and the Force dissipates, leaving you alone in the Dragon Stones.

After a moment or two, return to yourself.

Diary note, and a snack at least, some people like to have a gentle party.

Vernal Equinox
(Approximately March 19 to 21.)

Same 'rules' as before.

You stand, alone, in the pre-dawn night at the centre of the Dragon Stones, facing the trilithon in the East.

In turn you turn, acknowledge and pay your respects to the four Elemental Kings. Paraldar, King of the Air, in the East; Djinn, King of Fire, in the South; Neksa, King of Water, in the West; Ghobb, King of Earth, in the North. When these are all present you turn your attention to the altar and acknowledge and pay your respects to the Sovereigns of Faerie; King Oberon and Queen Titania.

When everyone is present, after a moment or two, you begin to rise through the atmosphere and out into space; there is no discomfort, all is gentle and peaceful.

You approach the Moon, pause and pay your respects, then continue on out into space.

Nearing the Sun you come to a halt and stand in space, feeling the Solar Winds flow passed you. You pay your respects to the Sun, then turn to face back the way you have come; waiting.

You become aware of a Beam of Sunlight coming from behind you and know that it is heading for Planet Earth.

As its leading edge passes, you step on and travel with it.

As the Beam enters the upper atmosphere it pauses, allowing you to send out the call to the sylphs of the Kingdom of the Air to awaken for the Spring.

The Beam moves on, taking you with it. It touches the Earth's surface and enters the planet, taking you down to the Fiery Core where it pauses for you to send out the call to the salamanders of the Kingdom of Fire to awaken for the Spring.

The Beam turns and heads back towards the surface, taking you with it. It emerges under the ocean where it pauses for you to send out the call to the undines of the Kingdom of Water to awaken for the Spring.

The Beam moves on, carrying you out of the sea, over a beach and into a mountain forest, where once again it pauses, allowing you to send out the call to the gnomes of the Kingdom of Earth to awaken for the Spring.

The Beam continues to wait for you to send out a further call to the Folk of the World of Faerie to awaken for the Spring.

You step off of the Beam and it departs to continue on its journey.

You stand in the Spring sunshine, soaking up the beauty of the forest; aware of the stirring activities of the Elemental Kingdoms and the World of Faerie and their ownership of Planet Earth.

You rise again into the air and fly back to the early morning Dragon Stones.

In reverse order, turning to the left each time, you pay your respects to those who have awaited your return. King Oberon and Queen Titania; King Ghobb; King Neksa; King Djinn; King Paraldar. They depart and you return to yourself.

Diary entry, a drink and a snack to finish.

Summer Solstice
(June 21.)

Whenever possible this rite should be conducted out in the open, with a clear view of a low, natural horizon. Carry it through in real time, at the actual sunrise.

Whilst you are still Working in the confines of the Dragon Stones, you do not have to see them; just be aware of their presence about you.

You are alone in the centre of the Dragon Stones, facing the Eastern trilithon.

You pay your respects to each of the following, turning to your right each time whereupon they are present in the Dragon Stones.

King Oberon and Queen Titania, the Sovereigns of Faerie, atop the altar.

Paraldar, King of the Air, in front of the trilithon.

Djinn, King of Fire, in front of the Southern pair of stones.

Neksa, King of Water, in front of the Western pool of water.

Ghobb, King of the Earth, in front of the Northern stones.

The Masculine stands in the trilithon.

The Dragon stands in the Southern stones.

The Feminine stands over the Western water.

The Senior Guardian stands between the Northern stones.

You finish up facing the point of the sunrise on the horizon, awaiting the first sign of the solar disc rising.

When it appears, you reach, mentally, for the Light as it crosses the Land and bend it around the circle of the Dragon Stones where it becomes a circle of spinning Light.

As the sun rises so more Light streams over the Land, adding to the spin and feeding it.

When approximately a half of the sun has risen, you begin to peel the Light from the inside of the spinning circle from the four cardinal points and draw it towards you and direct it into the ground beneath your feet.

You visualise these strips of light going to the heart of your Land, healing and cleansing therefrom.

As the Light enters the ground you call for the Change of Season; from Spring to Summer. The end of the phase of growth and the start of the ripening.

As the sun is just about to clear the horizon the circle of Light has gained its maximum momentum and the Light is streaming into the earth like a torrent.

The sun finally clears the horizon and you cut the flow from the sun to the Dragon Stones, whilst still continuing to peel the Light off the inside of the circle.

Eventually you have taken all the Light from the circle and poured it into the ground.

You pause for a moment or two to readjust yourself.

You turn to your left and begin to pay your respects in the reverse order to those who have been in attendance with you. Once acknowledged, they depart.

The Senior Guardian in the North; the Feminine in the West; the Dragon in the South; the Masculine in the East; King Ghobb in the North; King Neksa in the West; King Djinn in the South; King Paraldar in the East; King Oberon and Queen Titania on the altar.

Write up your notes and have a snack to ground yourself.

Autumn Equinox
(Approximately September 19, 20.)

You stand, alone, in the centre of the Dragon Stones under the night sky. The Moon has set and you can see the stars with the utmost clarity in the cloudless sky.

You adopt the 'Y' stance and invoke the Senior Guardian of your Land. A shimmering silver grey mist appears like a dome over the whole of the Dragon Stones. They are present.

Lower your arms and eyes and relax for a moment, before you pay your respects to each of the following, turning to your right each time whereupon they are present in the Dragon Stones.

King Oberon and Queen Titania, the Sovereigns of Faerie, atop the 'altar'.

Paraldar, King of the Air, in front of the trilithon.

Djinn, King of Fire, in front of the Southern pair of stones.

Neksa, King of Water, in front of the Western pool of water.

Ghobb, King of the Earth, in front of the Northern stones.

The Masculine stands in the trilithon.

The Dragon stands in the Southern stones.

The Feminine stands over the Western water.

The Guardian of Nature, Pan, stands between the Northern stones.

You finish up facing the trilithon and, once again, raise your arms into the 'Y' and invoke the Light to join with you.

From the depths of space; from the Stones; from everyone present, including yourself, and the very ground beneath your feet; comes a pulsing radiance, imbuing everything with a gentle brilliance.

You move to the altar. Looking down you see that between King Oberon and Queen Titania lying on the top of the stone is a single ear of wheat.

You ask their Majesties for permission to take it up, which they give.

You do so, gently and carefully, holding it in your cupped hands and move back to the centre.

You extend your arms with the ear of wheat in your cupped hands towards the King of Air. You give thanks for the winds that have blown across the fields, assisting in the pollination, regulating the temperature, all towards the growth and ripening.

You draw your arms back and turn towards the South, extending the ear of wheat towards the King of Fire. You give thanks for the heat and sunlight that has warmed the grain to bring growth and ripening.

You draw your arms back and turn towards the West, extending the ear of wheat towards the King of Water. You give thanks for the moisture that has fed the crop towards full growth and ripening.

You draw your arms back and turn towards the North, extending the ear of wheat towards the King of Earth. You give thanks for the nutrients that have been given by the earth towards full growth and ripening.

You draw your arms back and turn towards the East, extending the ear of wheat towards the Masculine. You give thanks for the wisdom inherent in the symmetry and geometry of the crop.

You draw your arms back and turn towards the South, extending the ear of wheat towards the Dragon. You give thanks for the earth energies that have coursed over the Land, stimulating the growth.

You draw your arms back and turn towards the West, extending the ear of wheat towards the Feminine. You give thanks for the powers that have come together under her guidance from above, below, and all sides to aid the growth.

You draw your arms back and turn towards the North, extending the ear of wheat towards the Guardian of Nature. You give thanks to nature for making it all possible, acknowledging that a single ear can produce fields of crops. Not just in your Land, but all over the world.

You draw your arms back and turn to face the trilithon.

You call to all present to acknowledge the symbolic single ear of wheat as a representation of all the fruits and crops of the earth. You ask that they be released in the harvest, accepting that a part of the harvest will be held for the new growth next year.

All present so acknowledge.

You raise your arms towards the silver dome of the Senior Guardian, offering the ear of wheat. This is accepted and the ear disappears from your hand, taken by the Force. Whereupon the Senior Guardian disappears and you lower your arms.

You pause for a moment or two to readjust yourself.

You turn to your left and begin to pay your respects in the reverse order to those who have been in attendance with you. Once acknowledged, they depart.

The Guardian of Nature in the North; the Feminine in the West; the Dragon in the South; the Masculine in the East; King Ghobb in the North; King Neksa in the West; King Djinn in the South; King Paraldar in the East; King Oberon and Queen Titania on the altar.

Write up your notes and have a snack to ground yourself.

Chapter 14

Vortices

As mentioned earlier, we are now going to move on to the second method of establishing a rapport with the Elemental Kingdoms. Previously we have dealt with each of the Elementals in a humanoid form (technically known as anthropomorphic representations), but we are now going to get nearer to the actuality of their existence by dealing with them as Vortices of Force.

Once again the Working environment is the Dragon Stones, but during the night rather than around the sunrise. We are going to be Working much more with colour and these tend to show that much better when shining in the darkness. You must be totally familiar with the Dragon Stones, so, if necessary, go back and run through Exercise 1 in Chapter 12 a few times to make sure that you are fully comfortable with them. Also, you should read through the various hints given in previous pages on getting yourself ready for Working. Even if you have decided to do the humanoid Exercises first, you can still benefit from doing the Exercises with the vortices. You can never know too much about the Elementals.

When you feel you are ready to make a start on these Exercises, read each one through a number of times to get the idea of what will be happening, what you will be required to do and in what order things need to occur. You could, of course, tape it and play it back to yourself.

A vortex? Imagine being in the bath, under the water, watching the plug being pulled. The swirling, spiralling water flowing down the plug-hole gives you an idea of what a vortex roughly looks like. All of the vortices will be spinning clockwise so the energy will be, as you look at it, coming in from your right, across in front of you, and away to your left.

At a certain point in each Exercise the vortex will communicate agreement to a request that you make. There is no definitive manner that this will be shown. For some it may be a pulse of bright light travelling down the vortex, for another it may be that the vortex will bow towards them, for someone else it may be something entirely different. You will soon recognise what is right for you.

Without any doubt I can promise you that, if you do these Exercises properly, you will undergo some interesting experiences.

Exercise 1: Air Vortex Merger

You stand in the centre of the Dragon Stones in the middle of the night, facing the Eastern trilithon. There is no moon, only starlight from the clear sky.

You direct your attention towards the trilithon and pay your respects to the Vortex of Air which appears golden between the altar and the trilithon.

You turn to your right and pay your respects to the other Vortices. The Vortex of Fire, red and orange, in the South; the Vortex of Water, blue, in the West; the Vortex of Earth, black, brown and dark green, in the North.

Once all are in place and things are harmonious, you turn your attention back to the Vortex of Air in front of the trilithon. You move forward, passing to the North of the altar stone and to stand near to the golden Vortex of Air.

Repeat your respects and ask for permission to approach closer.

(There may not be any response, therefore assume that things are not yet quite right for this to happen at this time so return to your central place and run through the closing shown later in this Exercise.)

When permission is granted you step forward to get comfortably close to the Vortex. Raise your PASSIVE hand (Left if right handed, right if left handed) and place it, gently, on the LEFT side of the Vortex as you face it, so that the energy runs under your palm from wrist to finger tips.

Get used to the feel of the vibration and, when you are comfortable with the sensation, lower your hand.

Look again at the Vortex and ask permission to enter.

When this has been given move a little further forward so that the Vortex is gently brushing against your chest and forehead. When you are comfortable with this, lean forward and RELAX.

Let the Vortex take you up into its spin and carry you in it's currents until it lowers you gently in the eye of the Vortex.

Once there, don't be in any hurry. Take things easily. Steady and orientate yourself so that looking out through the walls of the Vortex, you can see the other three Vortices in the Dragon Stones.

Relax and communicate with the Vortex in which you stand. Experience and understand the nature of the Element of Air. Realise what Air is about and what, esoterically, it carries with it.

Remember all these experiences as they are very important to you, and are unique to you.

(At some indeterminate point whilst Working with this Vortex you will be advised by the Vortex that it is time for you to leave this Vortex and, on your next daily visit, to turn your attention to the next Vortex. No one can tell how long this initial contact may require. It could be a day, a week, a month, or however long it takes the realisation to fully appear within you. The Vortex in question is the only judge.)

When the day's communication is over, the Vortex will reach in and lift you from the eye and take you back into its spin and gently deposit you back outside in the Dragon Stones.

Re-orientate yourself to stand, once again, facing the Vortex.

Raise your ACTIVE hand (Right if right handed, left if left handed.)and place it against the LEFT side of the Vortex as you face it, so that it is spinning under your palm from wrist to finger tips. Allow the EXCESS of Elemental Air that is now within your body to be drained off, re-stabilising yourself.

(This is action is imperative. If ignored you could find yourself in all sorts of problems in your daily life. Everyone has a certain amount of all of the Elementals within their bodies and they are in an harmonious alliance in regard to our Life and other philosophical themes. An excess of any of the Elementals within you can completely de-harmonise you and give rise to a wide variety of subjective destabilising sensations, which can be extremely disorientating and are not recommended.)

Offer your thanks to the Vortex and move, via the South of the altar stone, back to the centre of the Dragon Stones.

Turn to your left and begin the closing by paying your respects to each of the Vortices in turn. As you do so they disappear from your view.

The black, brown and green of the Earth; the blue of Water; the red, orange of Fire; and the golden Air.

You stand alone in the centre of the Dragon Stones and may, if you so wish, run through the Sunrise Exercise in the Dragon Stones, or simply return to yourself.

You have just undergone the first of many momentous experiences for you. Revel in it. Get it down on paper as quickly as you can after the event and as fully as possible. Don't be upset if words seem to fail you, that can be quite natural.

Above all, be honest with yourself. Your report is for your eyes only.

Make a note of you understandings of what has happened and of the realisation arrived at when it does.

Remember, it cannot be mind blowing every time. There may even be the occasion when nothing seems to happen at all. It is a wrong feeling, because something happens every time you enter, but some of the 'adjustments' are so subtle that they are beyond your immediate perception and you may only become aware of them after the passing of some little time. Just make the note that "Nothing appeared to happen". Then wait and see how things progress.

Don't forget the snack and a drink to ground yourself afterwards.

Exercises 2, 3 & 4: Fire, Water & Earth Vortices Mergers

The procedure for these mergers is exactly the same as with that of the Vortex of Air. The only difference is that you move directly to the new Vortex from the centre of the Dragon Stones. Normally there should be no doubt in your mind as to when to move on to the next Vortex. However, if you are unsure, one of two things may happen. Firstly, upon approaching the Vortex you have already been Working with, you will not be given permission to touch nor enter, so, simply pay your respects and move on to the next Vortex.

Secondly if in error you think that you have been told to move on, when you move to the next Vortex it will not respond to your requests. Don't be down-hearted, we all make mistakes. Remember, the person who never made a mistake never made anything. Simply move back to the previous Vortex and continue to Work with it. Don't be put off by apparent delays, curb your impatience, its not easy - I know that one. These delays may well pay a very high dividend in the future. Whilst the merge method is exactly the same, the difference with each Vortex lies in the

166

realisations and understandings received from the experiences.

Remember the stabilising active hand on the left of the Vortex.

Exercise 5: World of Faerie Merger
In the Dragon Stones as before, you pay your respects to the Elemental Vortices, who duly appear.

Face the altar and move forward to stand reasonably close to it.

Pay your respects and the two Vortices of Faerie appear on the top.

(The two Vortices, with all the colours of the rainbow in bars across them, represent the duality of the King and the Queen. The one on the right, as you face them, is the masculine with the red of the rainbow at the top, whilst the one on the left with the red at the base is the feminine.)

You advise them that the Vortex of the Earth has suggested that you should merge with the World of Faerie to complete your education.

You ask their permission to do so.

In response, the two blend together and form one larger Vortex, still rainbow barred, but the indigo is in the centre with red at both the top and the bottom. It moves forward and descends from the altar to spin in front of you.

Follow the same merger procedures as before with the Elemental Vortices.

When you have exited the Vortex, remember, active hand, left of the Vortex.

Pay your respects and the Vortex will return to the altar, separate and disperse.

Pay your respects to the Elemental Vortices and they disappear.

Sunrise if you wish, then return to yourself.

Diary, drink, eat.

Exercise 6: Working With The Vortex of Air

Having been advised by the Vortex of Faerie, and not before, you are deemed to be ready to begin to Work with the Elementals.

(Complete the previous Exercise procedures up to the point where you are standing in the eye of the Vortex of Air.)

Advise that Vortex of your intention to blend the energies of the Elemental Vortices.

Raise your ACTIVE hand and ease it through the spinning wall of the Vortex so that your hand is free outside the Vortex in the Dragon Stones.

Direct your fingers to point towards the Vortex of Fire in the South and call on the Air to go to the Fire.

You will see the golden light of the Air travel along your hand and arc across the space towards the Vortex of Fire. As it reaches the Fire you will see the golden light blend with the red and orange of Fire, enhancing that Vortex.

After few moments of this call for the energy to stop flowing, whereupon it will.

Redirect your fingers towards the Vortex of Water in the West and call on the Air to go to the Water.

You will see the golden light travel along your hand and arc across the Dragon Stones to the Vortex of Water. As it reaches that Vortex you will see the golden light blend with the blue and enhance that Vortex.

After a few moments of this call for the energy to stop flowing, whereupon it will.

Redirect your fingers towards the Vortex of Earth in the North and repeat the process. Watch the gold blend with black, brown and green, enhancing that Vortex.

After a few moments of this call for the energy to stop flowing, whereupon it will.

Turn your hand so that the palm is down and parallel with the ground and fan your fingers apart. Call on the Air to go to all three of the other Vortices at the same time. The golden light will move to your finger tips and arc out in all three directions; one to each of the others. You will see the gold blend with the natural colours of the Vortices, enhancing them all.

After a few moments call for the energy to stop flowing, whereupon it will.

Draw your arm back into the Vortex of Air and relax.

Wait awhile just in case the Vortex wishes to communicate with you. Make a strong mental note of any such input that you receive.

Then allow the Vortex to lift you out and return you to the Dragon Stones.

Re-stabilise yourself. Remember, active hand, left of the Vortex.

Back to the centre, via the South of the altar, and pay your respects to all the Vortices to release them. Turning to your left

The Sunrise if you wish.

Return to yourself.

Once again, the Vortex will tell you when to move on to the next Exercise. Things will be just the same as outlined in the earlier mergers.

Diary note, drink and a snack to get back into this world.

Exercises 7 & 8: Working With the Vortices of Fire & Water

The procedure for these two Exercises is exactly the same as Exercise 6, except that you move directly to the Vortex you are going to Work with.

The only differences will be in the colours flowing across the Dragon Stones and the communications received, if any.

Remember, active hand, left of Vortex.

Diary note, drink and a snack to ground yourself.

Exercise 9: Working With The Vortex Of Earth

The method of entry is exactly the same with the Vortex of Earth, however, it is what happens inside that is markedly different.

Heretofore when you have been within the Vortex you have broadcast that Vortex' energy to the other Vortices. This time you will be drawing the other Vortex energies to you.

Inside the Vortex of Earth raise your PASSIVE hand and ease it through the wall of the Vortex so that your hand is out, palm upwards, and free in the Dragon Stones.

Orientate your hand towards the East and the Vortex of Air. Call for the energy of the air and stretch for it. The golden energy arcs across towards your hand, through which it passes to blend with the Vortex of the Earth.

(Having previously merged with the Vortex of Air there should be no undue discomfort, although you might find it necessary to steady yourself as it strikes your hand. Allow the energy to flow naturally and just let things happen. Try not to get over involved with what is happening and try to remain as objective as you can.)

After a little while call on the Air to stop, and it does.

Re-orientate your hand towards the South and the Vortex of Fire. Repeat the call for the energy and pass the red orange energy to the Vortex.

After a little while call on the Fire to stop, and it does.

Re-orientate your hand towards the West and the Vortex of Water. Repeat the call for the energy and pass the blue energy to the Vortex.

After a while call on the Water to stop, and it does.

Re-orientate you hand towards the centre of the Dragon Stones.

Call to all three of the other Vortices for their energy, which arc into your hand.

(Once again, keep steady and let things flow naturally. Don't get involved and try to stay as objective as possible.)

After a moment or two call on the other Vortices to stop, and they do.

Draw your hand back inside the Vortex and relax.

Allow some time for the Vortex of Earth to pass any information to you, if it has any at this time. Remember it.

Then allow the Vortex to lift you out and go through the re-stabilising routine.

Remember, active hand, left side of the Vortex.

Close down as before and return to yourself.

Diary note, drink and snack to ground yourself.

Exercise 10: Working With The World Of Faerie

In the Dragon Stones, pay your respects to the Elemental and Faerie Vortices as before.

Merge with the Vortex of Faerie again.

Standing in the eye, raise BOTH of your hands over your head to be clear of the top of the Vortex.

Call for the energy of Faerie to go to the Elemental Vortices and four lines of rainbow coloured lights arc from your ACTIVE hand to them.

Once they are running calmly, call for the Elemental energies to come to the Vortex of Faerie. Four lines of the appropriate coloured lights come from the Elemental Vortices and meet with your PASSIVE hand for passage to the Vortex.

When all eight lines are stable let them run for a few moments then call for the Elementals to stop their flow, which they do, and then call on Faerie to stop also, which it does.

A pause for any input from Faerie, then ask to be released.

Outside the Vortex, re-stabilise and close things down as normal.

Diary notes, drink and snack.

Well, now you've done it! What happens next?

In the normal course of events the four Elementals, with the Sovereigns of Faerie, will sit down, so to speak, and evaluate all that has happened with you and how you have responded to both the Work and the individual Vortices.

They will decide how they can best use your unique qualities in the furtherance of Earth Healing. One of them will volunteer to be your mentor initially and lead you onward to meet and Work with any number of the numerous energies that are out there.

Congratulations and Welcome.

However, for those who wish, there is more.

Even though the course as such has come to an end and you are now in a position to make a very marked impact on the Earth Healing scene, there is always more that can be learnt. We are moving into a much more advanced stage of Working.

Heretofore you have been within an energy and acted as a channel for the energies to Work through. What we are now looking at is a much more personal involvement, in some respects you will be very much the objective magician, in others you will be transmitting your subjective energy to the cause.

In the centre of the Dragon Stones at night, neither moon nor clouds, facing the Eastern trilithon is our continued Working base start point.

Those Energies that were introduced in Chapter 13, Seasonal Rites, begin to take a more active part in what we are going to be doing.

Each of them has been colour coded so that you know exactly what you are doing. The Elementals and the World of Faerie have already been noted and Worked with.

The Guardian of Nature, Pan, caused me some problems until I left it to Pan to show me. It came up as black, flecked with red.

The Masculine Energy is amethyst, the Feminine Energy is blue and white, the Senior Guardian energy is silver grey.

The Dragon Energy, however gets a little complicated. It depends where you are.

For us in the United Kingdom the Dragon, or Pendragon as we refer to it, is scarlet. In the Americas the Dragon is pale green, flecked with yellow. In Iceland, the Dragon is gold.

If you should be somewhere else in the world you must needs check things out for yourself. Perhaps the best way is to acknowledge the presence of the Dragon and see what turns up. I can't help any more on that. Perhaps when I get to other places, I'll find out myself..

First Working

You stand alone in the centre of the Dragon Stones, facing the Eastern trilithon.

You lift your eyes to the night sky and pay your respects to the Senior Guardian of the Land. A silver grey dome appears over, and around, the entire Dragon Stones.

Lower your gaze to the top of the altar and pay your respects to the Sovereigns of Faerie. The two small rainbow Vortices appear on the top.

Look to the trilithon and pay your respects to the Air. The golden Vortex appears.

Turn to your right, face the Southern stones and pay your respects to Fire. The red, orange Vortex appears.

Face the Western pool and pay your respects to Water. The blue Vortex appears.

Turn to the Northern stones and pay your respects to Earth. The black, brown and green Vortex appears.

Back to the Eastern trilithon and pay your respects to the Masculine Energy of the Land. The amethyst Vortex appears behind that of the Air.

Towards the Southern stones and pay your respects to the Dragon. The Vortex appears behind that of Fire.

Over the Western pool pay your respects to the Feminine Energy of the Land. The blue, white Vortex appears behind that of Water.

To the Northern stones to pay your respects to Pan, the Guardian of Nature. The black, flecked with red, Vortex appears behind that of Earth.

Back to facing the East, you welcome them all as twelve representatives of your worlds, co-existing in harmony.

You raise your arms into the 'Y' and invoke the Light. A shaft of brilliance, originating somewhere in the unknown depths of space, descends and cuts through the dome to come down around you personally.

You welcome the Light.

Facing East, call for the Wisdom of the Air to go to the Land. A line of golden light arcs from the Vortex of Air to rise to join the Light where it intersects the dome of the Senior Guardian. The gold blends with the silver grey of the dome.

Facing South, call for the Energy of Fire to go to the Land. A line of red, orange light arcs up to join the Light where it intersects the dome. The red, orange blends with the gold and silver grey in the dome.

Facing West, call for the Power of Water to go to the Land. A line of blue light arcs up to the intersection in the dome, where it blends with the red, orange, gold and silver grey in the dome.

Facing North, call for the Mediation of the Earth to go to the Land. A line of black, green, and brown light arcs up to the intersection, blending with the other colours in the dome.

Facing East again, call for the Masculine Wisdom to go to the Land. A line of amethyst light rises to the intersection and joins with the other lights blending in the dome.

Facing South, call for the Dragon Earth Energies to go to the Land. A line of light goes to the intersection of the Light and the dome, to blend with the other colours in the dome.

Turn to the West and call for the Feminine Power to go to the Land. A line of blue and white light rises to join with the others and blends in the dome.

Facing North, call for Nature to go to the Land. A black flecked with red light emerges and rises to join and blend with the others in the dome.

Turn your attention to the twin Vortices of Faerie and call for the Faerie Energy to go to the Land. Two lines of rainbow coloured light rise to join the others and blend in the dome.

You step backwards, out of the pillar of Light, towards the West. You move back until you are the same distance from the Light as the twin Vortices of Faerie on the altar in the East.

Settle yourself, then raise both your arms and point all your fingers towards the intersection.

Offer your own energy to the Land. A fine line of opaque energy runs from the end of each finger and thumb to the intersection of the Light and the dome.

After a few seconds pause call for the Light to go to the Land.

The multi-coloured dome becomes a Dome of Pure Brilliance, washing all the other colours from your view.

You call for the Healing, Restoration, Unification and Evolution of the Land through the alliance of these Energies.

Stand for a while wrapped in the reflected purity of the Light.

Stop your energy flowing and lower your arms before walking forwards, back into the pillar of Light.

Pay your respects to the Faerie Sovereigns, who respond by stopping their energy flow and disappearing from your view.

Turning to your left you pay your respects to each of the Energies, who stop their energy flow and disappear from your view. Pan, the Feminine, the Dragon, the Masculine, Elemental Earth, Elemental Water, Elemental Fire, Elemental Air.

Raise your gaze to the shining dome of the Senior Guardian, pay your respects and watch the dome dissipate.

Stand for a few moments in the midst of the shaft of Light; the Light may wish to communicate with you. If it does, remember.

Raise your arms into the 'Y' and, as you do so, the Light rises and withdraws back into the depths of space from whence it came.

You stand alone in the Dragon Stones, which are humming gently to themselves.

If you feel the need, watch the sunrise.

Back to yourself.

Diary note, drink and a snack.

There has been a tremendous amount of energy flowing about you, even if you haven't been immersed in it. There is bound to be some residual energy wafting about. There is no way to drain off the energies by touching a Vortex as before.

There are two little actions which will help you to re-stabilise yourself.

Firstly, write up the most detailed and accurate account of everything that you experienced in this Exercise.

Secondly, at the very least, turn the cold tap on and let the water wash over your hands and wrists. If you have the time go and have a shower or bath or better still in an appropriate environment a swim or splash in the naturally flowing waters of a river, stream or lake. Obviously, before you start getting wet, have a quiet word with the appropriate energies asking them to help you get yourself back in order. Let the water carry the excesses away.

Don't be impatient. Work with this First Working until the Light tells you to move on. If you are not sure about moving on, don't. Stay with this until it does become obvious.

Second Working
You are now going to get a little more personally involved with what is happening.

(Complete the previous Working up to the point where the Light has arrived and you have welcomed it.)

Walk forward a pace or two towards the East, out of the Light and stop.

Bring your passive arm, palm facing the front, forwards from your side until it is a little over a foot from your hip; at an angle of between 30 and 45 degrees from your body.

At the same time, raise your active arm, palm forwards, over your head, also at an angle of about 45 degrees from the vertical.

When comfortable call for the Wisdom of the Air to come to you. The golden light arcs across to your passive hand, where it holds steady for a few seconds, then bounces up to your active hand. Once again it steadies itself.

You call for the Wisdom of the Air to go to the Land, whereupon it leaves your active hand and rises to the intersection of the Light and the dome.

The arc of golden light now runs from the Vortex of Air to your passive hand, then up to your active hand, and then up to the intersection, where it blends with the silver grey of the dome.

After a minute or so, advise the Vortex of Air that you are going to remove your hands. Having done so, release the arc and drop your arms. The line of golden light snaps up to go directly to the intersection.

Turn to your right and walk around the pillar of Light to stand and face the South.

Repeat the actions with your arms, and call for the Energy of Fire to come to you; which it does.

Complete the actions as before, then move on around the pillar of Light stopping at each of the Vortices and carrying out the procedures as before. The coloured energy light to you, then to the intersection, then direct to the intersection. Water; Earth; Masculine; Dragon; Feminine; Pan.

Arriving at the East, standing in front of the Sovereigns of Faerie, you extend your passive hand and raise your active as before.

When you call for the Faerie Energy, TWO lines of rainbow light come; one from each of the Vortices.

As the lines rise to your active hand they intertwine with each other to form a single line of rainbow light.

Complete the actions as before then walk around the pillar of Light to the West and out to your position, where you turn and offer your own energy as before to the Land.

In due course you call for the Light to go to the Land and all the other lights are washed from view in the dome.

Repeat your call for the Healing, Restoration, Unification and Evolution of the Land through the alliance of these Energies.

Stand for a while wrapped in the reflected purity of the Light.

Stop your energy flowing and lower your arms before walking forwards, back to the pillar of Light, then move around the South of it to the East to face the Sovereigns of Faerie. Pay your respects and they stop the flow and disappear from view.

Move to your left and go around the pillar paying your respects to each of the Vortices in turn, whereupon they stop broadcasting their energy and disappear from view.

Pan; the Feminine; the Dragon; the Masculine; Earth; Water; Fire; Air; the Senior Guardian.

When you are alone move into the pillar of Light.

Stand for a few moments in the midst of the shaft of Light; the Light may wish to communicate with you. If it does, remember.

Raise your arms into the 'Y' and, as you do so, the Light rises and withdraws back into the depths of space from whence it came.

You stand alone in the Dragon Stones, which are humming gently to themselves.

If you feel the need, watch the sunrise before returning to yourself.

Diary note, drink and a snack. The fullest detail in your report and a rinse, wash, shower, bath, dip or a swim. You will need it more and more as you get deeper into the energies.

If the Light has advised that it is possible for you to move on, if you so wish, you come to the last of our little Workings.

Final Working

It doesn't matter what anyone else might say about your readiness for this step, listen to that still, small voice within. YOU have got to feel RIGHT about this. Read it through. See what you're letting yourself in for. Have a serious think about it. Then decide.

BE WARNED, YOU ARE 'PLAYING WITH FIRE', DON'T WRECK YOUR LIFE, REMEMBER PERSONAL RESPONSIBILITY.

(Complete the First Working up to the point where you have welcomed the Senior Guardian and the Vortices are in their positions about the Dragon Stones, but don't call for the Light.)

Standing in the centre of the Dragon Stones you call to the Sovereigns of Faerie for Faerie Energy.

The two Vortices drop down off of the altar and move towards you. As they do so they are joined by a number of tiny rainbow Vortices. They all move to encircle you a yard or so from your feet. From the Faerie Ring comes lines of Faerie Energy rainbow lines to set a clockwise turning circle about your feet.

You call to the Air for that Energy and the line of golden light crosses to join and merge with the Faerie Energy about your feet.

Turn to the South and call for the Fire Energy. The red, orange line of light joins the others about your feet, blending with the other Energies.

Turn to the West and call for the Water energy. The blue light joins and blends with the others about your feet.

Call for the Earth energy. The black, brown and green light joins and blends with the others about your feet.

Call to the Masculine Energy to join the others about you. Then the Dragon, the Feminine, and Pan.

You are now stood with the nine energies flowing freely, clockwise, about your lower legs.

You raise your arms into the 'Y' and invoke the Light. A shaft of brilliance, originating somewhere in the unknown depths of space, descends and cuts through the dome to come down around you and the Ring of Energy about your feet.

You lower your arms and welcome the Light.

You call for the Healing, Restoration, Unification and Evolution of the Land through the alliance of these Energies.

As you make this call you raise your arms back into the 'Y', which draws the Energy Ring from about your lower legs, over your body and over your head to rise to meet the silver grey dome, where the multi-colours wash through and blend with the dome.

You stand cocooned in the multi coloured lights and let your own opaque energy run from your finger tips up to the dome.

Call for the Light to go to the Land. The encircling brilliance pulsates and all the varied coloured lights of the Energies are washed from the dome in the indescribable brilliance of the Light.

You lower your arms and let the Energies continue to flow about you for a short while.

Turning to your left, within the Energy Ring, you pay your respects to each of the Energies, who stop their energy flow and disappear from your view. Pan; the Feminine; the Dragon; the Masculine; Elemental Earth; Elemental Water; Elemental Fire; Elemental Air; the World of Faerie.

As each disappear, their particular Energy flow stops and the cocoon about you thins.

When all have disappeared and all their Energies have risen from about you, take some time for yourself. Stand for a few moments in the midst of the Light; it may wish to communicate with you. If it does, remember.

Raise your arms into the 'Y' and, as you do so, the Light rises and withdraws back into the depths of space from whence it came.

You stand alone in the Dragon Stones, which are humming gently to themselves.

If you feel the need, watch the sunrise.

Back to yourself.

Diary note, drink and a snack.

The fullest detail in your report. Each and every detail must be fully and totally grounded.

A rinse, wash, shower, bath, dip or a swim will help.

No human being, living or dead, can guide you any further. You have boldly gone beyond such realms. Whatever happens now, and where you go, who with and to do what, is down to the liaison and rapport you have established with the twelve energies you have made contact with.

To type 'Well Done' seems inadequate, but you will know what I mean.

Chapter 15

Evolution

I have constantly spoken of Changes throughout these pages. Now that you have Worked your way through the various exercises you are hopefully beginning to come terms with your own position in the Greater Scheme of Things.

Both The Merlin and Cheiron went to a great deal of trouble to instil the knowledge in us that we each are a very small cog in a very, very large machine. If that very small cog doesn't operate correctly then the whole machine, no matter how large it may be, will not operate to full efficiency nor capacity. Planet Earth is somewhat sick at this time and needs all the help it can get in order to get well and continue along its predetermined course of evolution. No, I don't know where that course is leading us.

One of the many Creation Myths tells us that mankind was seeded from another planet. Cheiron would neither confirm nor really deny such a happening, but he did make the point that if we were so seeded then surely the longer term objective would be for us to move on, ever outward and to colonise other planets. The problem was, as he intimated, that we would need to understand what we were doing to Planet Earth and rectify it before we would be allowed to move up and out. We had to clean up our own backyard before we would be allowed to mess up somebody else's yard.

Perhaps it was coincidence that when we were opening the envelope and pushing for the other planets in our solar system that suddenly almost over night everything stopped. No longer was there anything in the press about probes going to this or that place.

All the space exploration nowadays seems to be centring on satellites and experiments in the space lab.

Being in that frame of mind, I wondered if, perhaps, the Unseen Guardians had put a serious stop to such things because we hadn't got our act together as yet. However, I must admit that I have not received any input to suggest that this is so or not.

The only space related input that I have received to date has been concern by my advisors about the network of satellites that are circling the Earth. They maintained that even if those satellites didn't necessarily communicate with each other, their mere presence was creating a form of electronic web about the whole of the planet which was not conducive to some of the incoming, essential off planet energies. That problem has now been dealt with and the web neutralised.

Back here on *terra firma* metaphysically over the passed few years there have also been some changes. In the Earth Healing Chapters I stressed the point that permission had been granted by the Elemental Kingdoms to use the Ancient British placements about the Dragon Stones no matter where you might be in the world. However very early in 1990 I had taken a trip to Derbyshire and made my first acquaintance with the pivotal stone circle of Britain, Arbor Low. As I had walked in I had made my usual greeting to the Guardian of Place and received the extremely stern commandment that whilst I was welcome I was not under any circumstances to do anything. As I had wandered in I had found that the energies within the circle were all to pot. Positives and negatives were all out of line and totally out of synchronisation. I had left more than somewhat puzzled.

As the conversations with Cheiron had progressed he had told us that the re-alignment within those stones were a part of new phase and, slowly but surely, he led us to come to the understanding that where we had always had Air in the East; Fire in the South; Water in the West and Earth in the North, the new mandate was to be Fire in the East; Earth in the South; and Air in the North. Water remained where it has always been, the West. I actually put it to the test in the Swinside Circle in the

Cumbrian Lake District in Northwest England. Instead of walking the Circle from East, to South, to West, to North I had acted on the information received from Cheiron that we should now be looking at walking the circle in what we were to come to term as the Lightning Wheel. I had entered from the West (a place of Wisdom or Knowledge), across to the East (a place of Enlightenment), then down to the South (a place of Trust and Innocence), and on up to the North (a place of Instruction), then back to the West (having, ostensibly, added to my sum of Knowledge) and therefore ready to walk the Lightning Wheel again and move on in my instruction. As I had left the circle there had been a pleased, congratulatory rumble from the Guardian of Place that someone, at last, had recognised the change of emphasis.

As we had doodled with pad and pencil, drawing the shape had alerted us to the fact that we were beginning to look at the sign for infinity - a figure 8 on its side - a lemniscate. Continually walking the Lightning Wheel would lead us to infinity?

Whilst not going back and actually Working with the Elementals as I had done before I did check it out with them and they were in full agreement with these changes in placements. We have continued to Work with these positions and the lemniscate ever since without any problem or query by any of the Guardians.

You now have the Knowledge of what is going on, take it to those of the Management that you are Working with for verification or Enlightenment, Trust in what you are Learning and walk the Lightning Wheel towards even more Knowledge and so the Path moves ever onward.

I am reminded that you can lay the Major Arcana of the Tarot Journey of the Fool into the lemniscate, which would be a graphic portrayal of this concept.

What follows is an attempt to show the 'map', 'path', however you want to see it, that June and I have walked. We are here, and adjudged to be, relatively, sane, or as sane as anyone can be in this crazy world of Planet Earth. We have been there. There is nothing to fear. So, step boldly forward and go see what is 'out there'. Not as a favour, but simply because, whatever it is, you have the right to the knowledge and no-one can ever deny you.

Chapter 16

A 21st Century Qabalah?

As I have said earlier, no one can tell you where you may go beyond the Vortices of Energies that we have mentioned in these pages. All I can offer is a list of the Energies that we have contacted - a sort of map if you like. Remember you are a unique individual and your map may well be markedly different, however I offer this map simply as an indication of the immense possibilities that could be open to you. I have used the directions of North (N), South (S), East (E), and West (W) as a simple guide to where each Vortex 'stands' in the Wheel even though as we rise such a direction is totally alien to the level concerned. I ask you to accept that the names given are purely names of convenience in order to help us to have some sort of understanding of what we are dealing with at any given point or level

There is no compulsion to follow it to the end, you may stop wherever you feel comfortable.

We start at the bottom in order to gain a sense of perspective, starting from things that we know before we leap into the unknown.

Level 1   **The Divine Spark**
That animating aspect within us all.

Level 2   **The Individual**
Existing within the persona :   Mind (N); Wisdom (W); Spirit (E); Physical (S).

Level 3   Spiritual Awareness
Guardian Angel (N); Sensitivity (W); Awareness (E); Understanding (S).

Level 4   The World of Faerie
Wings (N); Queen Titania (W) - Rainbow, Red Base;
King Oberon (E), Rainbow - Red Pinnacle; Gate (S).

Level 5   The Elemental Kingdoms
King Paraldar (N) - Air - Gold; King Neksa (W) - Water - Blue;
King Djinn (E) - Fire - Red, Orange; King Ghobb (S) - Earth
Black, Brown, Green.

Level 6   National Archetypes
Senior Guardian (N) - Silver Grey; Feminine (W) - Blue, White;
Masculine (E) - Amethyst; Dragon (S) - National Colouring.

(Britain - Herne the Hunter (N); The Lady of the Lake (W); The
Merlin (E); The Pendragon (S) - Scarlet.

Iceland - Eagle (N); Bull (W); Giant (E); Dragon (S) - Gold.

Americas - Masàw (N); Grandmothers (W); Grandfathers (E);
                Dragon (S) - Pale Green flecked Yellow.)

Level 7   International Archetypes
Planetary Being (N) - Grey flecked Silver; Lunar (W) - Silver;
Pan (E) - Black flecked Red; Earth Dragon(S) - Rich Green.

Level 8   Solar System
Sun - Creator (N); Uranus - Destroyer (W); Saturn - Harmony (E);
Pluto - Mover (S).

Level 9   Cosmos
Orion (N); Ursa Major (W); Pleiades (E); Ursa Minor (S).

Level 10   Guardians
Source of Perceived Light (N); Law, Form (W); Mind, Force (E);
Prism (S).

Level 11   Nameless, Faceless Ones
Indescribable : Archetypal models as shown in the Tarot Aces.
Swords (N); Cups (W); Wands (E); Pentacles (S).

Level 12   The Pantheons
The Veil of the Unmanifest (N); The Goddesses (W); The Gods (E);
The Unity of Gods and Goddesses Combined (S).

Level 13   The Great Unmanifest
A Total Conscious Sense of Unity and Being.

Level 14   Within The Great Unmanifest
Indescribable.

As an added assistance, I have drawn a simplified Diagram of
these Levels over the page.

There is a knowing that there is more, but we have yet to find it.
Tarot logic suggests that there are twenty two levels. We must
wait and see what turns up; good hunting!

The Key to all Doorways, the remover of all blockages and
impediments is held in a simple stanza. Think seriously, however,
before you claim your right to such knowledge. The latter part
obligates you still further.

I NEED TO KNOW, IN ORDER TO SERVE!

May Your God Go With You,

Geoff,
October 1996

A 21st Century Qabalah Diagrams

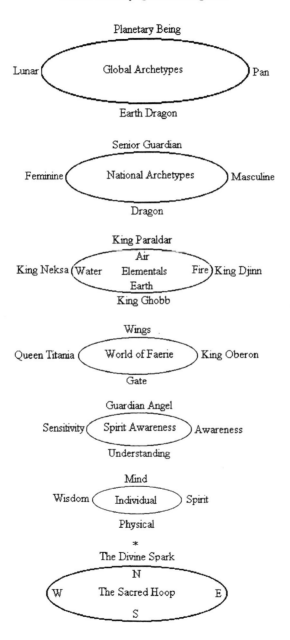

Planetary Being

Lunar　Global Archetypes　Pan

Earth Dragon

Senior Guardian

Feminine　National Archetypes　Masculine

Dragon

King Paraldar

Air

King Neksa　Water　Elementals　Fire　King Djinn

Earth

King Ghobb

Wings

Queen Titania　World of Faerie　King Oberon

Gate

Guardian Angel

Sensitivity　Spirit Awareness　Awareness

Understanding

Mind

Wisdom　Individual　Spirit

Physical

*

The Divine Spark

N

W　The Sacred Hoop　E

S

191

Within The Great Unmanifest

The Great Unmanifest

Veil To The Great Unmanifest

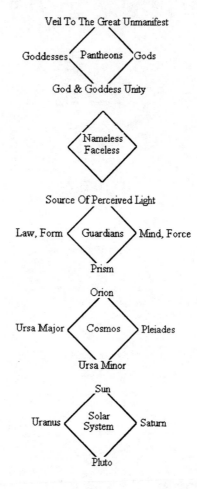

Goddesses Pantheons Gods

God & Goddess Unity

Nameless
Faceless

Source Of Perceived Light

Law, Form Guardians Mind, Force

Prism

Orion

Ursa Major Cosmos Pleiades

Ursa Minor

Sun

Uranus Solar System Saturn

Pluto

Having Assimilated All The Earth

Energies, We Move Into More Rarified Things.

192

Chapter 17

Afterword

In closing I would like to draw your attention to the Native American Black Elk and his vision at the end of the 18th century. He advised that he saw all the peoples of the world walking the Sacred Hoop; red, brown, black, yellow and white people.

Many have taken this to mean that everyone should look to the Native American Medicine Wheel and, for a time, so did I, however, I have since come to the conclusion that this is not so.

Whilst we are beginning to come to an understanding of the global view of the interplay between us all, we have to acknowledge that many of the disciplines of what we do are suited to the geographical area, the psychology of the peoples concerned and the nations in which they proliferate.

For instance, Islamic peoples don't eat pork. In the area of North Africa where the Prophet spoke the Word it would probably have been very difficult to stop such meat from putrefying and poisoning the eater. Perhaps there is something similar in the Indian sub-continent with beef.

Westerners make a great deal out of the Tibetan Singing Bowls. If you look at what they have in Tibet you would soon see why they are metal and not wooden bowls. There is a very severe shortage of trees from which to get the wood to make them, whereas there is a great deal of ore in those mountains from which to manufacture something to hold a bowl of rice.

Bhuddists are renowned for their Prayer Wheels and are constantly turning them.

Hindu men and women in India are ever walking the Wheel of Life.

Spiritualists sit in Circles for development of their abilities.

Wiccans cast their Circles to Work.

Story-tellers prefer to weave their web in the midst of a Circle of listeners.

The Chinese have long used the ancient art of Feng Shui for the positive placement of articles in their homes. Although it is presented as an octagon, it doesn't take much imagination to see that it is a Circle in the same way as the others.

Here in Pagan Britain we have our Stone Circles.

Everywhere we look we find the symbol and image of the Circle.

That I believe is the Sacred Hoop to which Black Elk was referring.

Enter your Circle and help the World to spin in it's circular (elliptical?) orbit; become a Sun Dancer, Stimulate and Dance the Dreamtime Sacred Hoop Awake.

Secret Places of the Goddess By Philip Heselton

This book is a practical and evocative encouragement to seek the Earth Spirit in those special places where it dwells, embracing a wide definition of Paganism to include all those inner yearnings towards a closer contact with the land. It will appeal to all who are drawn to visit such natural and archetypal locations in the landscape as tree groves, sacred springs, special rock outcrops, the seashore and the Wild Wood. All these are Secret Places of the Goddess.

The author shows why certain locations have been considered numinous and magical and how we can each go about finding these special places in the landscape. He provides a vision of the variety of ways in which we might respond to the spirit present at such sites and thereby enter into a closer relationship with the Old Ones.

ISBN 1 898307 40 7   £10.95   190 pages

Lost Cities and Sunken Lands by Nigel Pennick

Revised and updated 2nd edition
Nigel Pennick has gathered together the rare fragments of literary, pictorial and folklore remains detailing information on the remains of lands around the British coast which have been destroyed by the sea. The roll-call of these lost lands and sunken cities, and the fate of once thriving coastal towns such as Dunwich and settlements such as Caer Arianrhod and the lost Lowland Hundred of Cantref y Gwaelod, challenges us to reconsider whether the lost land of Lyonesse, which once extended from Land's End to the Scilly Isles, existed solely in Arthurian legend.

ISBN 01898307 83 0   £10.95

Sacred Geometry Symbolism and Purpose in Religious Structures

By Nigel Pennick
Geometry underlies the structure of all things - from galaxies to molecules. Despite our separation from the natural world, we human beings are still bounded by the laws of the universe. Each time a geometrical form is created, an expression of this universal oneness is made & from the dawn of time religious structures have expressed this unity in their every detail. In this absorbing history, the first of its kind, the applications of sacred geometry are examined & the full extent of its practise is revealed. Sacred geometry is responsible for the feeling of awe generated by a gothic cathedral & the 'rightness' of a Georgian drawing-room. Sacred Geometry traces the rise & fall of this transcendent art from megalithic stone circles to Art Nouveau & reveals how buildings that conform to its timeless principles mirror the geometry of the cosmos.

ISBN 1 898307 156   £9.95   190 pages

Sacred Animals by Gordon Maclellan

This is a book about animals, animals to wonder over in the Otherworld and in this physical world. Communicating, organising a sacred space, using words and chants, finding totems, the use and making of masks and costumes, body paints, music and dance are all part of communicating with animal spirits. These are all described here together with practical issues such as conservation and the integration of magic, ritual and practical hands-on action. Gordon communicates his love and wonder of animals, and of life with the enthusiasm and vitality for which he is widely known - a brilliant book full of practicality and feeling.

ISBN 1 898307 69 5   £9.95

FREE DETAILED CATALOGUE

A detailed illustrated catalogue is available on request, SAE or International Postal Coupon appreciated. Titles are available direct from Capall Bann, post free in the UK (cheque or PO with order) or from good bookshops and specialist outlets. Titles currently available include:

Animals, Mind Body Spirit & Folklore
Angels and Goddesses - Celtic Christianity & Paganism by Michael Howard
Arthur - The Legend Unveiled by C Johnson & E Lung
Auguries and Omens - The Magical Lore of Birds by Yvonne Aburrow
Book of the Veil The by Peter Paddon
Caer Sidhe - Celtic Astrology and Astronomy by Michael Bayley
Call of the Horned Piper by Nigel Jackson
Cats' Company by Ann Walker
Celtic Lore & Druidic Ritual by Rhiannon Ryall
Compleat Vampyre - The Vampyre Shaman: Werewolves & Witchery by Nigel Jackson
Crystal Clear - A Guide to Quartz Crystal by Jennifer Dent
Earth Dance - A Year of Pagan Rituals by Jan Brodie
Earth Harmony - Places of Power, Holiness and Healing by Nigel Pennick
Earth Magic by Margaret McArthur
Enchanted Forest - The Magical Lore of Trees by Yvonne Aburrow
Familiars - Animal Powers of Britain by Anna Franklin
Healing Homes by Jennifer Dent
Herbcraft - Shamanic & Ritual Use of Herbs by Susan Lavender & Anna Franklin
In Search of Herne the Hunter by Eric Fitch
Inner Space Workbook - Developing Counselling & Magical Skills Through the Tarot
Kecks, Keddles & Kesh by Michael Bayley
Living Tarot by Ann Walker
Magical Incenses and Perfumes by Jan Brodie
Magical Lore of Cats by Marion Davies
Magical Lore of Herbs by Marion Davies
Masks of Misrule - The Horned God & His Cult in Europe by Nigel Jackson
Mysteries of the Runes by Michael Howard
Oracle of Geomancy by Nigel Pennick
Patchwork of Magic by Julia Day
Pathworking - A Practical Book of Guided Meditations by Pete Jennings
Pickingill Papers - The Origins of Gardnerian Wicca by Michael Howard
Psychic Animals by Dennis Bardens
Psychic Self Defence - Real Solutions by Jan Brodie
Runic Astrology by Nigel Pennick
Sacred Animals by Gordon MacLellan
Sacred Grove - The Mysteries of the Forest by Yvonne Aburrow
Sacred Geometry by Nigel Pennick
Sacred Lore of Horses The by Marion Davies
Sacred Ring - Pagan Origins British Folk Festivals & Customs by Michael Howard
Seasonal Magic - Diary of a Village Witch by Paddy Slade
Secret Places of the Goddess by Philip Heselton
Talking to the Earth by Gordon Maclellan
Taming the Wolf - Full Moon Meditations by Steve Hounsome
The Goddess Year by Nigel Pennick & Helen Field
West Country Wicca by Rhiannon Ryall
Witches of Oz The by Matthew & Julia Phillips

Capall Bann is owned and run by people actively involved in many of the areas in which we publish. Our list is expanding rapidly so do contact us for details on the latest releases.

Capall Bann Publishing, Freshfields, Chieveley, Berks, RG20 8TF Tel 01635 46455